JUST A LOVING TOUCH
By Simon Bamford

CHARACTERS *in order of appearance*

CATHY

Cathy is a young woman in her mid twenties. She is very attractive. Very confident with a selfish determination.

TONY BANKS

Tony is also in his mid-twenties. Of average build, clean shaven. He is a lively, cheerful man.

SAM PICTURE

Sam is a man in his fifties. Slim. A kind man. Very patient with a certain wisdom usually found in older people. Sam is a male nurse but, at no time during the play does he appear in uniform.

MILLY BANKS

Milly is in her fifties. She is of average build. Milly is suffering a memory disorder... This is not apparent at the beginning of the play, only in a humorous fashion.

BILLY BANKS

Billy is in his fifties. A round build. A rather pompous man, full of self importance. In his pursuit to impress others he fails to impress those closest to him. Milly, for example, is an irritation to him with her forgetfulness. He also has a dark secret that he hides very well, but not completely.

HEATHER PICTURE

Heather is in her mid-twenties. She is an attractive girl but in the beginning of the play she does nothing to enhance this. She is slender and has shoulder length hair. She is a sad figure. A victim of Poliomyelitis during her childhood that has left her with a lame leg. She has a quiet tenderness and shyness but not a complex about her lameness.

ACT I Scene 1

The action takes place in the lounge of a terraced house. There are two entrances. One leads to the hall and stairs, and another leads to the kitchen and back door. Spread over the floor is a dust sheet. On the dust sheet is an erected pasteboard. On the pasteboard a teapot, an electric kettle, two mugs, a carton of milk, a bag of sugar and half a packet of digestive biscuits. Under the pasteboard is a bucket containing paste and a brush. In the middle of the room is a tea chest containing various pieces of wrapped chinaware, covered by a square of plywood. A set of step ladders lean against the wall. The only other furniture in the room is an easy chair covered with a dust sheet.

CATHY, a good looking girl in her mid-twenties, is sitting on the tea-chest drinking tea from a mug. She gazes idly at the wall above the mantel. She is dressed in a tee-shirt and jeans. She stands, places the mug on the pasteboard, looks closely at the wall above the mantel, shakes her head in disapproval. She moves to the window. Looks at her watch. Shakes her head, sighs, turns, picks up the mug, sits and resumes drinking.

TONY enters. He is also in his mid-twenties. He wears almost the same clothes as Cathy but his are paint splattered. Tony is a cheerful, energetic man. He carries five rolls of pale blue wallpaper.

TONY: Hello darling.

CATHY: Hi.

TONY: Been here long? *(Puts wallpaper onto pasteboard. Lightly kisses her)*

CATHY: About an hour... There's tea in the pot.

TONY: Pour me one... Got the paper for the "Loving room".

CATHY: Loving room?

TONY: Bedroom.

CATHY: Oh. *(Pours tea)*

TONY: Hope you like it... Here, is that cup clean?

CATHY: No. Doesn't matter... It's not poisonous.

TONY: Wash it up.

CATHY: It's yours!

TONY: Makes no difference. Tip it out. Wash it up.

CATHY: I hope you're not going to be this fussy when we're married.

TONY: I'm sensible, not fussy.

CATHY: Oh God, you sound just like your mother. *(Exit)*

TONY: *(Opens roll of paper)* This was a real bargain. Only two ninety-nine a roll. Twenty five per cent off.

CATHY: *(Enters)* One mug. Sterilised.

TONY: *(Unrolls the paper)* Like it?

CATHY: *(Pours tea)* No.

TONY: It's nice. Twenty five per cent off.

CATHY: It's off all right.

TONY: *(Sulking)* Well perhaps if you could help pick things instead of leaving it all to me, then perhaps you may get something that suits.

CATHY: *(Coldly)* Tea. *(Hands him mug)*

TONY: Ugh... It's cold.

CATHY: So's that paper. Be like sleeping in an igloo. All that blue. I told you pink.

TONY: They didn't have pink.

CATHY: Rubbish. The shops are full of pink paper.

TONY: *(Angrily rolls up the paper)* Right, I'll take it back. Get pink. If that's what you want, pink it will be.

CATHY: Good.

TONY: Make fresh tea.

CATHY: Make it yourself. I have to go soon.

TONY: Go? You've only just arrived.

CATHY: I'm meeting Jean. Going shopping. And I may point out, I have not just arrived, I've been here over an hour waiting for you.

TONY: Oh. *(Pause)* As you're going out you can take the paper back and get pink.

CATHY: I'm not walking around all day carrying five rolls of wallpaper, thank you.

TONY: It's on your way. Only take five minutes.

CATHY: But I'll have five pink rolls to cart about won't I?

TONY: Yes, but...

CATHY: No "but" about it.

TONY: I think it's about time you started taking an interest in this place. Good God, we've only got three weeks and you don't seem to want to do anything but stroll around the shops with Jean.

CATHY: *(Snaps)* Hang the bloody stuff. I don't care.

TONY: *(Shouts)* Make up your mind. You said you didn't like it.

CATHY: *(Shouting back)* Well I do now.

TONY: *(Sulking)* Only because it's too much trouble. Dead lazy you are.

CATHY: No I'm not. *(Sighs. Speaks tenderly)* Let's not fight. *(Kisses him)* Premarital tension, I expect. Perhaps it will look better when it's up.

TONY: You sure?

CATHY: Sure.

TONY: Not too cold?

CATHY: Well. Yes. But never mind, I expect you'll keep me warm.

TONY: Care to go up now? *(Puts arm around her)* I'll hold it against the wall. You can see how it hangs. You'll love it once you see it up.

CATHY: *(Pulls away)* If you think I'm falling for that one you've another think coming.

TONY: *(Sighs)* Suppose not. What with you suffering premarital tension. *(Pause)* And what about this room? Does this meet the required high seal of approval?

CATHY: It's all right, I suppose. Not sure about that paper over the mantel. Bit dark.

TONY: God, there's no pleasing you is there?

CATHY: Well you should know, lover boy.

TONY: That sounds like a complaint.

CATHY: If the cap fits.

TONY: *(Snaps)* Are you going to make that tea or what?

CATHY: No. I have to go. Jean hates to be kept waiting.

TONY: *(With anger)* Jean! Jean! Who cares about Jean? You should be caring about this place. I need help. I've so much to do and there's not enough hours in the day.

CATHY: *(Shouts)* Well you'll get nothing done by sitting around drinking tea, will you? Typical British workman, that's you. Can't do bugger all unless the kettle's on.

TONY: And you do nothing but tart around town all day with Miss La-de-da Jean. Wonder you don't think about marrying her instead of me.

CATHY: I'm off. I've better things to do than stand around bickering with you.

TONY: *(Grabs the kettle, moves to kitchen exit)* I'll make my own tea.

CATHY: Good. Nice to see you getting started at last. *(He glares at her. She blows him a cheeky kiss. He sticks his tongue out at her then exits. She calls through)* If I see some nice pink paper I'll buy it.

TONY: *(Entering quickly)* What about the blue?

CATHY: Stick it over the mantel. *(Exit laughing)*

TONY: *(Calls loudly)* Pity you don't stick La-de-da Jean over the mantel. *(Cathy is heard to laugh)* If you don't, someone should... and it might just be me. *(Moves to kitchen)* Yes it might just be me. *(Exits)*

A knock on front door. A pause, a louder knock.

SAM: *(Off)* Hello.... Anyone at home?

SAM PICTURE enters. SAM is about fifty. He is of average build. Dressed in blue overalls. He carries a teapot and two mugs.

Hello.... Hello.... Anyone about?

TONY enters.

TONY: Hello... Yes, can I help you?

SAM: Hello... I knocked twice. Door was open. Hope you don't mind me barging in?

TONY: No. But who are you?

SAM: Sam. Sam Picture. I'm your neighbour. Passage side. I had a cuppa on the go. Thought you might like one...

TONY: Thanks. Very thoughtful of you.

SAM: Yes. I know what it's like working alone. Too busy to stop and make one.

TONY: Actually, I was about to...

SAM: I always have a cuppa at this time, I thought why drink alone. Also a chance to introduce myself...

TONY: Well, yes, thanks. Sit yourself down. There's mugs on the.... Oh, I see you've brought your own.

SAM: Yes. I thought perhaps you hadn't had time to unpack yet. Shows how wrong you can be about people. *(Begins to pour tea)* Where's the little woman off to then?

TONY: Little woman?

SAM: Your soon to be!

TONY: Oh, you mean Cathy. Gone out. Shopping.

SAM: Thought it was her. Saw her going up the road.

TONY: Down the road.

SAM: No. Up. You take sugar?

TONY: Yes. Thanks. Two. She's going up the city so she must have gone down the road.

SAM: *(Hands him tea)* Well when I saw her she was going up. Definite.

TONY: Couldn't have been her.

SAM: Oh it was her all right.

TONY: You know her?

SAM: Not to speak to. I've seen you both coming and going over the last few weeks or so.... I expect you're thinking I'm nosy... I'm not really... Just like to know what's going on around me..... Round here it's best to keep yourself to yourself.... So, when's the big day then?

TONY: *(Smiles)* Three weeks Saturday.

SAM: So soon?... Better start conserving your energy. You'll need it being.... married. *(Sits)*

TONY: How long have you been....

SAM: Married?

TONY: Yes.

SAM: I'm not... Well, not now.... but I was.

TONY: Sorry.... Divorced?

SAM: Divorced?.... No, son.... She passed on two years ago.

TONY: Sorry.

SAM: It was cancer.... very painful.... Very drawn out it were.

TONY: I'm sorry.

SAM: *(With a soft casualness)* Again, no need son... But thanks all the same....
Two years is a long time... You get over these things... Tell you the truth I was
glad when she finally went... Six years I watched her suffering... Six painful
years watching her turning into a yellow empty skin of decaying flesh... Funny
world this... If she had been an animal that I allowed to deteriorate into that
state, well there's no saying what they would have done... Slapped me in clink
I expect... The worst bit were the times I just sat looking at her. Feeling
useless.... It was her eyes.... I can never forget her eyes... If I had a gun I would
have willingly blown her brains out.... Her eyes would ask me to..... But I didn't
have a gun.... Or the courage.... *(Suddenly cheerful)* But life goes on.... You
make the most of what you've got... I don't thank the Lord for taking her, but I
do thank Him for my time with her.

TONY: Sorry. It's sad to lose someone you love.

SAM: Love son? Hah. What is love? People spend their lives taking each other for
granted, getting on each other's nerves, shouting at one another over stupid
things. And there are times when you hate each other so much you wonder what
you've done to deserve each other... Nobody realises the capacity of their love
until they see it slowly fading away... The poets say, "The joys of love". Well
you're not aware you were joyful until it starts to hurt... God, I sound like some
Greek freak spouting on about the mysteries of life. *(Coughs, picks up
wallpaper)* This for in here?

TONY: No... This room is finished.

SAM: Oh, sorry. Thought it might be for over the mantel.

TONY: It's for the bedroom.

SAM: Bit cold don't you think, for the bedroom?

TONY: No. I happen to like it... Mind you, Cathy doesn't. She wants me to change
it... for pink.

SAM: Yes. Pink's better. For the bedroom. Blue's cold. Is that what you were
fighting about?

TONY: Fighting?

SAM: Heard you through the wall. Like paper they are. Be warned. The old gal other side spends all her time with her ear to the paper.

TONY: So, I expect, like you, she heard our quarrelling?

SAM: Don't take offence old son. Nothing you can say or do will shock me. And what I hear, or see, will go no further... But her next door, well, spends half her time on the gate, yapping.

TONY: Thought you said she spent her time with her ear to the wall?

SAM: Half her time! Other half reporting what she knows. Old Mother News of the World. That's what they call her.

TONY: Well look, I really must get on.

SAM: Anything I can do to help?

TONY: No. Thanks. I'm sure you must have lots to do yourself. Can't be easy living alone.

SAM: Oh but I don't live alone old son. What made you think that?

TONY: Sorry... I... Sorry, but I thought....

SAM: Now, don't you go jumping to conclusions. I haven't got some fancy bit... I have a daughter.

TONY: Daughter? Oh, yes, of course.

SAM: Heather. Expect you'll bump into her soon enough.... Not that she goes out much, but I expect you will.... Now are you sure I can't give you a hand?

TONY: I can't do much anyhow... My mum and dad will be here soon.

SAM: Oh, I see. Don't want to be in the way, so best I leave you to it then. *(Moves to the hall exit)* Now, don't forget, if help's needed, just knock on the bedroom wall. Or you could pop round. Have a cuppa. Perhaps meet Heather.

TONY: Yes. Thanks. I will.

SAM: I'll say good day then. See you later. *(Exits)*

TONY: *(Picks up the wallpaper. Looks at mantel)* Don't know what they mean, dark? I think you're lovely. *(Looks at blue paper)* Cold?... Not cold.... blue's fresh.... and as I'm the only one who's bothered about anything going up then it will have to be left to my taste.... That's the trouble, too many people around today without taste, imagination, designer flair. *(Looks at mantel)* Suppose you could have been a shade lighter. *(Looks at blue paper)* Wonder if you would look better over the mantel?... If I put you upstairs and she comes home with pink... Can't put pink over the mantel. *(Throws himself into the easy chair)* Why does everyone keep interfering?... *(Looks at pasteboard)* He's forgotten his teapot and mugs... I'd better take them back... Stop talking to yourself Tony Banks. People will think you're crackers... Well, who else is there to talk to?... I'd rather talk to myself... *(Stands. Picks up teapot and mugs)* At least I can get a word in... Oh no you can't... Oh yes I can. Oh no you can't. *(Moves to door)* Can. Can't. Can. Can't. God, I'm going nuts. Wish I'd brought my radio. Wish I'd stayed in bed. Wish I'd...

MILLY BANKS enters. She is a woman in her fifties. She is dressed elegantly, in blue. At this point in the play she is slightly scatterbrained and forgetful with a lightness that does not make these failings to be of concern.

MILLY: Hello John. Where's Tony?

TONY: Hello Mum. And it's Tony, not John.

MILLY: Oh, is it. Of course it is. Where's John?

TONY: John's not here. Should he be?

MILLY: Of course he should. I suppose he's out drinking again and him with so much to do, only three weeks to go, or is it three months?

TONY: It's three weeks and it's not John who's getting married, it's me, Tony.

MILLY: *(Inspecting room)* Is it? Yes of course it is. I'm always getting you boys mixed up. My age I expect... Where's your father got to?... Oh, you've made tea.

TONY: Well I was about to, but then this bloke...

MILLY: Well wash those mugs before you do. I won't have tea from a dirty mug.

TONY: I'll have to make fresh. The pot's empty.

MILLY: But you said you've just made one for this bloke. What bloke? Where's your father?

TONY: Oh never mind... Did you bring the paint?

MILLY: Paint? What paint?

TONY: Oh no Mum. I asked you for some brilliant white.

MILLY: Did you?

TONY: Yes. You said Dad had some in the shed I could have.

MILLY: Can't say I've ever seen any.

BILLY BANKS enters. BILLY is also in his fifties. He is a portly man, smartly dressed. He has a tendency to be self-important. A very proud man. He carries a tin of brilliant white gloss paint.

BILLY: Good morning son. I've brought the paint you asked your Mother for. Ah, you've made tea. *(Places the paint onto the pasteboard)*

TONY: Thanks Dad, and no. The pot's empty.

BILLY: Could do with a cup. Out at home. Your Mother forgot to buy some.

TONY: I'll put the kettle on.

MILLY: I'll do it John. And give me those cups. They need to be washed. *(Takes mugs and teapot, exits)*

TONY: Mother's memory is getting dreadful.

BILLY: Yes... Making a good job in here son. Almost professional. Didn't know you had it in you. What are you going to put over the mantel?

TONY: *(Irritated)* It's already over the mantel.

BILLY: Is it? Bit dark, don't you think?

TONY: No... Yes... It's trendy.

BILLY: Don't know about trendy. Looks dirty.

MILLY enters

MILLY: Sorry about being late John. It was your Father's fault. He forgot to remind me.

TONY: It's Tony!

MILLY: I distinctly told him I promised to be here at nine and he forgot. Men. Their brains are different to ours. It was his fault we forgot the paint.

BILLY: *(Holding up the paint)* Paint!

MILLY: Only because I reminded you. *(Exits)*

BILLY: You know, there are times when she drives me bonkers.

MILLY enters.

MILLY: And by the way, I don't like that paper over the mantel. It's too dark. *(Exits)*

TONY: *(Shouts)* No it's not. It's not too dark. I happen to like it even if you don't.

MILLY enters

MILLY: Don't you shout at me young John.

TONY: *(Still shouting)* It's trendy. Modern. And it's Tony. And Tony likes it. Everyone has it now-a-days.

MILLY: Well we haven't John. *(Exits)*

TONY: *(Almost in a tearful fury)* It's Tony. It's Tony. And Tony's sick of it. Sick, do you hear? Sick of people coming round here just to criticise. *(Sits sharply down onto tea chest)* Oh God I'm so sick of it.

BILLY: Just premarital tension I expect , son.

TONY: It's not tension. It's depression. Deep, dark depression. It seems I've spent my life in this house trying to reach the end of this bloody decorating... Cathy's always out... I never see her. And when I do... she doesn't like this, doesn't like that, doesn't want this, doesn't want that... I'm so tired. I'm working night and day... A man needs his comforts... I sometimes think it would be better if I were gay and she were a bloke, at least I'd have the satisfaction of punching her in the mouth... She doesn't like the house... Don't like the street. Don't like the mantel. Mantel's too dark. Blue's too blue.

BILLY: Blue?... Blue's too.... What blue?

TONY: Paper on the table. She thinks it's too cold for the bedroom.

BILLY: *(Picks up the paper)* Yes. She's right. It is a bit cold... *(TONY glares)* For the bedroom.... *(TONY stands angrily)* I suppose you could always...

TONY: *(Storming to the kitchen)* I know. I know. Stick it over the mantel.

BILLY: Oh dear... we're all entitled to our opinion... Definitely too cold. *(Puts wallpaper down. Places hand on brow, thinks deeply for a moment)* Now lets see.... My dear Lady Chairman.... Or is it Chairperson?... My dear Lady Chairperson. Your Grace, Members of the Council, ladies and gentlemen... Or is it, Your Grace, my dear Lady Chairperson, Members of the Council, ladies and gentlemen. I, William Anthony Banks, would like to express my feelings. No. Deep feeling of honour to be seen fitting in your eyes to be selected this year as the Right Honourable...

MILLY enters.

MILLY: Have you been upsetting young Tony? How many sugars do you want?

BILLY: The same as for the last twenty nine years. None. And no. I have not been upsetting young Tony.

MILLY: Well someone has. He's through there now ranting and raving about the only person who's offered to help him is some man who knows a woman who was in the News of the World. And who were you talking to?

BILLY: I was not talking to anyone.

MILLY: I'm beginning to worry about your sanity Billy Banks. Talking to yourself. Been doing that quite a lot lately.

BILLY: I was rehearsing my...

MILLY: Think I'll have a word with Doctor Ellis about you next time I'm in. *(Exits)*

BILLY: *(Loud)* I was rehearsing my speech, you stupid... Oh God, what's the use.... Your Grace, Lady Chairperson, Members of the Council, ladies and gentlemen... I would like to start by saying that many years ago when I was a lad. And when I say many years ago, I mean many years ago... Laughter. Laughter. Laughter... Ha-ha-ha. Ha-ha-ha.

MILLY enters with two mugs of tea.

MILLY: Now it's laughing at yourself is it? Here. Your's is the one with two sugars.

BILLY: I was rehearsing for tonight... I don't take sugar, you know perfectly well...

MILLY: You said two!

BILLY: I did not!

TONY enters with a mug of tea. He sips it.

TONY: Agh. No sugar.

BILLY: That's mine. Your mother has yours.

BILLY takes the mug from Tony. TONY takes the mug from Milly. MILLY sits in the easy chair. TONY sits on the tea chest. BILLY moves over to the tea chest.

BILLY: Here. Wiggle your bum over. *(Sits with Tony. After a short silence of tea blowing and sipping, BILLY speaks)* I still think....

TONY: Don't say it. Just don't say it.

A short silence.

MILLY: I wonder if she was on the front page?

BILLY: What are you talking about?

MILLY: This woman. She was in the News of the World.

BILLY: Why?

MILLY: Probably had an affair with a politician. *(To Tony)* Did she dear?

TONY: No. What I said was... Oh never mind I'm not in the mood to go into all that again.

BILLY: I'm getting lost here.

MILLY: Pressed her up against the wall by her ears apparently.

BILLY: *(Stands and faces them)* Would one of you dear people please enlighten me as to what we are talking about?

TONY: It's nothing. Just a joke the man this side made about the woman that side.

BILLY: A joke? Was it rude?

TONY: No.

BILLY: I could do with a joke for my speech tonight.

MILLY: What speech?

BILLY: Oh God. How could she have forgotten tonight?

MILLY: I thought it was next week.

BILLY: Oh give me strength. Tonight you and I are going to the Town Hall, remember?

MILLY: And you're giving a speech. Why?

BILLY: *(Proudly)* The newly elected Lord Mayor always gives an acceptance speech.

MILLY: But you may not be elected.

BILLY: Who else? Who else?

MILLY: Arnold Bunn!

BILLY: Arnold Bunn? Arnold Bunn? No chance. No chance. Heavens he's no competition. I mean. What's he done? Go on, you tell me.

MILLY: No less than you.

BILLY: What? He hasn't been around more than five minutes, whereas I've been loyal to the party for thirty five years.

MILLY: Your Father forced you to join.

BILLY: Well yes. But that's not the point. I've given my life to Socialism. Look how I've fought to push local issues through. My astounding success in forcing the council to adopt pedestrian walkways in the city centre. Just think of the respect I've won from the public on that one issue.

MILLY: The motorists hate it.

BILLY: But the pedestrians love it.

MILLY: The shopkeepers hate it.

BILLY: *(Angry)* But the pedestrians love it.

MILLY: According to the shopkeepers, most of the pedestrians are going elsewhere, in their cars. Too far to walk to the car park, they say.

BILLY: Nonsense.

MILLY: So why do we shop out of town then?

BILLY: Because...

MILLY: Because it's too far to walk to the car park that's why.

BILLY: Now look here. When you wake up in the morning you'll be the Lady Mayoress of this fine city, so best you wake up without this negative attitude of yours.

MILLY: And on the other hand I may wake up as plain old Mrs Milly Banks and thank God for it.

BILLY: What? What?

TONY: Oh for God's sake Dad, let it drop.

BILLY: I was hoping you'd all be very proud.

TONY: Of course we're proud Dad, but you're not there yet and we won't think any the less of you if you don't get it.

BILLY: Oh but I will. You mark my words, I will.

CATHY enters.

CATHY: Oh, hello Mum, Dad. How are you?

BILLY: Hello my sweet.

TONY: Thought you were out for the day.

CATHY: I need the Building Society book.

TONY: Why?

CATHY: I need some money.

TONY: Why?

CATHY: To give away to beggars of course. What do you think I need money for?

TONY: I don't know, that's why I'm asking.

CATHY: Look, this is getting on my nerves. I suppose you think it's some kind of picnic running around all day buying this, buying that, seeing to everything. You've been no help.

TONY: *(Shouts)* No help? No help? I've been locked up in this hole for the last three weeks trying to get it finished. And what have you done? What have you done?

CATHY: I'll tell you one thing I've done and that's to say I'll marry you, but we're not married yet.

TONY: You can say that again.

BILLY: Now come on children...

CATHY: Keep out of this Pops. And don't call me a child. *(Turns on Tony)* And what have you done? Every time I walk through that door you're sitting drinking tea.

MILLY: Would you like a cup?

CATHY: No.

MILLY: Going to buy your dress dear? Won't be long now.

CATHY: I bought the dress two months ago. I told you. *(Hisses)* Tony will you get me that book.

TONY: No.

MILLY: What colour?

CATHY: White of course.

MILLY: That's nice. White's nice.

CATHY: *(Aside)* Of course it's white, stupid woman.

TONY: Don't call my Mother stupid.

MILLY: I got married in.... Married in... What colour did I get married in Billy?

BILLY: White.

MILLY: Did I?

BILLY: Yes dear you did. *(To Cathy)* But it could have been cream, pink, pale blue, it doesn't have to be white. All my wife asked you was what colour. There was no need for you to be rude.

CATHY: *(Sighs)* But she's the one who's been going on about a white wedding for months on end. If I had my way it would have been a registrar wedding and the money we saved could have been used to pay someone to get this place finished by the year two thousand.

MILLY: It's just your nerves. I was like that. Found fault with everything and everyone.

CATHY: I am not nervous, just irritated... Tony... Get me that book.

BILLY: But you couldn't even think of a registry wedding, not now.

CATHY: Why not?

BILLY: Well, tonight it's almost certain that I shall become Lord Mayor.

CATHY: *(Uninterested)* How exciting.

BILLY: Be out of the question the son of the Lord Mayor getting wed in the registrar office. Has to be a big do. Think of the publicity. You'll be famous.

CATHY: *(Laughing)* Famous.

BILLY: Yes, the daughter-in-law of the Lord Mayor of Norwich.

CATHY: *(Mocking)* Oh yes, I can see it all now. The famous Cathy Banks... No... No, silly me... People will stop calling me Cathy. I expect it will be "Hello. How are you? Wife of the son of the Lord Mayor of Norwich." And I suppose next year when your term of office is over, they'll say, "Hello. How are you? Wife of the son of the Lord Mayor of Norwich, last year or the year before."... Now Tony. Get me that book. I'm in a hurry.

TONY: It's packed away somewhere upstairs. I don't know if I can find it.

CATHY: Well go and look, please. It shuts in an hour.

MILLY: Come on John. I'll help you look.

TONY: Mum, my name's Tony. *(To Cathy)* And when I come down I want to know what you want the money for. Understand? *(They exit)*

A silence.

BILLY: I sometimes wonder where your values lie, young woman.

CATHY: Values?

BILLY: Oh you can adopt that attitude if you like, but once you're a member of this family you'll soon start to learn.

CATHY: Is that a fact?

BILLY: Yes. And I'm going to take a great delight in being your teacher.

CATHY: You? What the hell do you think you can teach me?

BILLY: Values young woman. The values of Socialism.

CATHY: Socialism?

BILLY: I'm a Socialist and proud of it. Born and bred a Socialist. My Mother and Father fought for the movement. Would have laid down their lives if necessary, and likewise, I've raised my family by the same principles. There's no finer code than the values of Socialism.

CATHY: Values my arse.

BILLY: Tone down that mouth of yours, young lady.

CATHY: *(Laughs and curtsies)* Oh of course, I forgot. One has to watch one's "P's" and "Q's" when one is speaking to the Lord Mayor. The Socialist Lord Mayor.

BILLY: How dare you?

CATHY: Easy. Freedom of speech. Isn't that a part of Socialism too? Along with equal rights for all? Bring down the rich? Equality of wealth... All people should have an equal share.

BILLY: There's nothing wrong in that, young woman.

CATHY: Unless of course you happen to serve on the council. Then it's the same for everyone except you because you deserve a bit more than the man on the street.

BILLY: You talk nonsense.

CATHY: No. Not a bit more. A bloody great chunk more. And you're a fine example of Socialism. Tonight, here in your fine Socialist controlled city, people without a roof over their heads will be queuing up outside the Night Shelter or the Sally Army for a bed and a bite to eat. And you live on Newmarket Road. Five bedrooms. Two of you? Where's the equality in that?

BILLY: How on earth my son landed himself with someone like you I'll never know.

CATHY: Easy... He walked into the Conservative Club and picked me up.

BILLY: The Conservative...?

CATHY: Yes that's right. He walked right in. They don't do a body search and

"Show us your ID" like they do at the Labour Club.

BILLY: He went to the Conserva...

CATHY: Yes. He waltzed in, picked the first Tory tart he fancied. And that Buster, is how he landed himself with me.

BILLY: My God, if you're an example of the Tory rank and file femininity, then all I can say is thank God for Maggy Thatcher.

The argument has now reached shouting level. The following lines are spoken to overlap. During the argument TONY rushes in and dances about in panic "Shushing" them until they fall into a silence, glaring at each other.

CATHY: Yes. Good old Maggy.

BILLY: The destroyer of human rights.

CATHY: Rubbish. Rubbish. Rubbish. The best thing...

BILLY: Taxes are higher in real terms.

CATHY: Twenty five per-cent down from thirty three and third per-cent.

BILLY: Not in real terms.

CATHY: Rubbish.

BILLY: V.A.T. up to fifteen per-cent.

CATHY: Prices more stable than ever before.

BILLY: Inflation up.

CATHY: Wages gone through the roof.

BILLY: Over three million on the dole.

CATHY: Less than two million.

BILLY: Falsified figures... Statistical evidence proves there are over three million people out of work.

CATHY: But not on the dole. You bloody Socialist's call a man with no arms or legs fit for work.

TONY: Shush. Shush. Shush. Good God. Good God. The walls. The walls. Like paper. Like paper.

CATHY: What are you on about Tony? I told you I don't like the paper.

TONY: The walls. Like paper. The neighbours.

BILLY: Neighbours?

TONY: Yes. Yes. Both sides. Spend all their time pressing their ears to the wall. It's their hobby. So stop it. Stop it.

A silence.

BILLY: You never told me you went to the Conservative Club, Tony.

CATHY: Went? He's a member.

BILLY: What? Is this true? Is this true, Tony?

TONY: Yes, it's true.

BILLY: What?

CATHY: So hang that on your chain of office.

BILLY: If this gets out - oh God, the scandal. What on earth possessed you to join that place?

TONY: The beer's cheaper.

BILLY: Beer! Beer! Is that all you think about? Have you no respect. You'll have to resign.

CATHY: He's fully paid up for the rest of the year. And you don't resign, you just forget to pay your dues. *(To Tony)* Did you find that book?

TONY: Yes. Here. *(Hands her the Building Society book)*

BILLY: I forbid you to set foot in the place again.

CATHY: The Lord Mayor has spoken.

TONY: The only place I'd like to step into is the street. Haven't seen daylight for weeks. And you said you were going to help me Dad.

BILLY: Well I can't do anything in these clothes. I have to keep up appearances. Can't be seen walking around in working clothes. Be reasonable.

CATHY: And I expect you've got writers cramp from signing autographs.

TONY: Shut up. You're no better. Always out. Out with La-de-da all the time. I need help and I need it now.

CATHY: Who do you think you're talking to?

TONY: I'm talking to you. The girl I'm supposed to love. The girl I'm supposed to be marrying.

CATHY: Well don't bother. *(Storms out)*

TONY: Now look what you've done.

BILLY: She'll come back, though I'm beginning to wonder if you'd be better off if she didn't. What on earth made you choose a Conservative?

TONY: I love her, Dad.

BILLY: Beats me how anyone could love a Conservative.... Where's your mother?

TONY: Upstairs.

BILLY: I don't understand how you found your way into that club. What's she doing up there?

TONY: Looking out of the window... I told you, the beer's cheaper and the music's better.

BILLY: Music's good down the Labour... Why should she want to look out of the window?

TONY: Said she felt funny.... And another thing, the Conservative Club is run by the Young Conservatives, not old foggies like the Labour. "Take your partners for the next foxtrot".

BILLY: Nothing wrong with the foxtrot. Lasted longer than your "jumping up and down throwing a fit" dance... Go and tell her to hurry up. I need a dickie-bow.

TONY: *(Goes to the stairs, calls)* Mum. *(Pauses)* Are you all right up there?

MILLY: *(Off)* Is that you Tony?... Why aren't you at school?... Playing truant again, you naughty boy.

BILLY: What did she say?

MILLY: *(Off)* But these aren't my sheets... No these aren't mine.

TONY: Mum?... Mum?... *(No response)* Something's wrong. *(Exits)*

BILLY: Tell her to hurry up. *(Picks up wallpaper)* Blue!... Typical Tory taste... Don't know why she dislikes it so. Expected the whole house to be blue, with a portrait of Thorn Faced Thatcher over the mantel.... Your Grace, My dear Lady Chairperson, Members of the Council, ladies and gentlemen, as your newly elected Lord Mayor of this fine city, I would like to say how proud I am to have the honour of placing a bomb under number ten Downing Street. I feel it is my duty to all mankind to rid this land, once and for all, from the tyranny of Toryism.

TONY enters. He is concerned.

TONY: Dad, there's something wrong... She's talking to herself.

BILLY: She always talks to herself.

TONY: Dad, listen will you... She thinks I'm just home from school.

BILLY: Pay no attention. She has these little dreams. They happen all the time.

TONY: Dad, she's ill.

BILLY: No. She's just tired... She always does that when she's tired... You should hear her talk in her sleep.

TONY: Dad, listen, I think you should get a doctor.

BILLY: Nonsense.

MILLY enters.

MILLY: Those bedrooms are just like the one's in Barrack Street.

TONY: Mum... Are you all right?

MILLY: Of course. Why shouldn't I be?

TONY: Upstairs you were talking as though it were ten years ago.

MILLY: Was I?

TONY: Yes.

MILLY: Brought back memories of Barrack Street those rooms.... I was happy in Barrack Street.... I expect I was daydreaming... I can't remember.

BILLY: See. I told you so.

TONY: But...

BILLY: I told you, sometimes she drives me bonkers. *(To Milly)* Now dear, I think we'd best be on our way.

MILLY: On our way?

BILLY: Yes. I want to buy a dickie-bow. For tonight.

MILLY: For tonight?

BILLY: Town Hall, remember?

MILLY: Oh yes. Town Hall. Thinking of Barrack Street made me forget. Silly me.

BILLY: Yes. Silly you. Now pick up your bag and let's be on our way.

MILLY: Did I bring a bag?

BILLY: How should I know?

MILLY: Did I have a bag when I came in John?

TONY: *No. And the name's Tony.*

MILLY: Yes, so it is.

BILLY: Goodbye son... Come on Milly. *(Exits)*

MILLY: *(Puts fingers on her eyes, then, as though in a trance, she kisses him)*
Now be a good boy John, and don't go leaving your toys all over for Mummy to clear up.

TONY: What?.... Mum...

She moves away. BILLY enters with a handbag.

BILLY: You stupid woman. You left it on top of the car. It's a miracle it wasn't stolen.

MILLY: See what I mean? Goodnight. *(They exit)*

TONY: *(Scratching his head)* Goodnight? *(Looks at watch)* It's only... God is that the time? *(Moves to the window. Waves. Turns, looks around room. He frowns)* I know your problem mantel... You're too stuck up... Get it? Too stuck up... *(Picks up blue paper. Sits)* And as for you, twenty five percent off. *(Yawns)* If I put you in the bedroom we'll all freeze to death... Could always buy a hot water bottle, I suppose. *(Yawns loudly)* God I'm tired... Working too hard I expect. *(To mantel)* Sorry pal... You're just not liked. Too dark, that's why... People don't like dark things... Won't admit it straight out... Don't want to appear racist... Don't think they fancy me any more either... No wonder... I stink of paint and paste... Spoilt all my nice, sexy, tight jeans... Look at these one's... Times were, as soon as I put them on, someone would want to rip them off... But that was long ago... Before I became a common painter and decorator. *(Looks at the blue)* Don't like you either... Us three, we're cripples. *(Yawns)* Social cripples. Suffering the same prejudices. *(Settles down into chair)* Touching our caps to our betters. Yes Guv... No Guv. Straight away Guv... Quick give me a flag. Here comes the Lord Mayor... Lord Mayor Banks... or Beadle of the workhouse... Looks the part. *(His eyes are getting heavy)* Don't worry you two... everything will work out. *(His eyes close)* They'll love you.... eventually.

The lights fade down to half light as he falls asleep. Play music to indicate the passing of time. A light tap on the door. He makes a nonsensical high pitched mumble. The knock is repeated, louder.

HEATHER: *(Off)* Hello... Mr Banks. Are you there?

HEATHER enters. She is a pretty girl. At this point, she appears rather plain, hair tied back, no make-up, dressed in trousers and an ill-fitting, old-fashioned blouse. She walks with a limp.

HEATHER: Hello. Mr Banks. *(She moves cautiously to him. Reaches out to touch his arm, declines, he mumbles loudly, She turns to leave)*

TONY: *(Awakes)* What... what... Yes what?

HEATHER: Sorry.

TONY: *(Reacts to her pale figure in the half light)* Aghh! God, who are you?

HEATHER: *(Nervously)* Sorry. Sorry. I didn't mean to wake you.

TONY: Who are you? What do you want? I thought you were a ghost. Frightened the life out of me.

HEATHER: Sorry... I live next door.... My Dad left our teapot and...

TONY: Oh yes, of course... You must be... be...Rosemary... Never forget a name.

HEATHER: Heather, actually.

TONY: Heather? Oh yes. Sorry. Knew you were a plant of some sort.

A silence.

HEATHER: *(Nervously)* Teapot!

TONY: *(Stands)* Oh yes, teapot. *(Looks at watch)* Is that the time? Half past five... I've been asleep since... Since... Since, God, I've done nothing. I'll be hung drawn and quartered!

HEATHER: You must be tired, working so late. *(He frowns. She is embarrassed)* I hear you through the bedroom wall.

TONY: Yes, I know... Teapot! Put that light on will you. *(Exits to the kitchen)*

HEATHER switches lights on, moves back to same position. TONY enters, hands her teapot and mugs.

HEATHER: Thank you. *(Turns away)*

TONY: You're welcome. *(Turns away)* Thank your Dad for me. It was thoughtful. Not many people bother now-a-days. *(Turns back)*

HEATHER: *(Turns, smiles)* Oh. Yes. Well, Dad's like that... Hope he didn't stop you working?

TONY: Stop me? I haven't even got started yet.

HEATHER: You deserve a rest.

TONY: Wish everyone thought like that. Cathy thinks that I...

HEATHER: *(Interrupting)* I like this room. It's lovely. Much better than it used to be.

TONY: Used to be?

HEATHER: Mrs Caxton. The lady who lived here before. I sat with her in the evenings.

TONY: Oh, I see.

HEATHER: Till she died.... Over there... by the fire.

TONY: Wish you hadn't told me that.

HEATHER: She would have like it now. Especially that paper over the mantel.

TONY: Would she? I should have married her instead.

HEATHER: *(Hesitates, smiles)* I like it too.

TONY: Do you? Do you really? God, you have a lovely smile. Haven't seen many smiles today... Or yesterday, or the day before that. And you like this paper? *(Laughs)* Will you marry me?... Sorry. Didn't mean to make you blush. Cathy hates it. My Mum hates it. So does my Dad and I don't think your Dad is struck on it either... They think it's too dark. I love it.

HEATHER: So do I.

TONY: I was beginning to think I was strange or something. *(Picks up blue wallpaper)* They suggested I covered it over with this.

HEATHER: That's pretty. I'd like that colour in my bedroom.

TONY: That settles it. You must marry me... Oh, I'm sorry but I forgot to empty that teapot.

HEATHER: Doesn't matter. I was about to make another.

TONY: So was I.

HEATHER: Oh. So you'll be needing...

TONY: No. I have one of my own.

HEATHER: Oh. But Dad thought...

TONY: Yes I know. Strange he didn't know. Wall being so thin.

HEATHER: Yes. It's terrible. It's worse on the other side. At least down here we have the passage way between us, that helps. Upstairs you can hear when someone turns in their sleep.

TONY: Upstairs? Oh dear... You said the old lady died in here? I was wondering if anyone ever managed to give birth?

HEATHER: Sorry, but I don't understand.

TONY: Conception! Conception can be very noisy I believe. *(Laughs)* Well I know mine is. Who sleeps other side of the wall, front room?

HEATHER: My Dad. Don't worry. Dad's a nurse.

TONY: Oh... So he'd spot the difference between labour pains and conception pains. Don't want him rushing in with a pan of hot water do we... A nurse is he? Can't imagine him in black stockings.

HEATHER: Silly... He's a male nurse.

TONY: No.

HEATHER: They do exist... And contrary to popular belief, male nurses do get married, to women, and have children. Some of them are quite normal.

TONY: I like your sense of humour. Same as mine. But I can't say the same for your Dad. He doesn't like my mantel.

HEATHER: *(Laughs)* Well no. He does tend to be rather old-fashioned, but he's a dear. He means well.

TONY: I'm sure he does. You'd better hurry or we'll have him knocking on the wall for his tea.

HEATHER: He's not there. He's on duty. Shift work. Sometimes nights so that should ease your mind. I was going to make tea for myself.

TONY: Tell you what. Why don't we share a pot?

HEATHER: Well.... I... But... I....

TONY: Don't be shy. I'm not going to eat you. Remember I'm the neighbour now and with only a sheet of paper to divide us, I expect I'll soon be like one of the family. I'll put the kettle on.

HEATHER: I'll do it.

TONY: I'll show you where.

HEATHER: I know where it is. I've been here before remember. *(Moves to exit)*

TONY: *(Casually)* Hurt your leg?

HEATHER: *(Stops abruptly)* Yes.

TONY: What you been doing? Falling down the stairs?

HEATHER: No. It was a long time ago... Polio. Poliomyelitis. *(Exits)*

TONY: *(Slaps hand to face)* Blast. Blast. Blast. Me and my big mouth. *(Moves to exit, hesitates, returns into room, takes top off tea chest, removes pieces of chinaware. Places two cups and saucers onto pasteboard)* May as well drink out of decent cups... Me and my big mouth.

CATHY enters. She looks worried.

CATHY: Hello Tony.

TONY: *(Moves to kiss her)* Hello. Didn't expect to see you.

CATHY: *(Moves away)* Don't. You'll regret it.

TONY: What's wrong? Not still sulking about this morning, are you?

CATHY: *(Turns away)* No.

TONY: If you're wondering what I've done today, well the answer to that is, nothing. I fell asleep.

CATHY: It doesn't matter.

TONY: Pardon?

CATHY: Not any more.

TONY: Well it certainly mattered this morning. What was the date you gave me for it's completion? Year two...

CATHY: Tony. I must talk to you. *(Turns)* I have something that you must know about.

TONY: Don't tell me you're...

CATHY: No... Don't be stupid... I don't know how to say this... It's difficult... I know you'll go crazy... But it's for the best. *(Turns to mantel)*

TONY: What's for the best? I know. You've decided that paper has to come down. *(Laughs)*

CATHY: No... Tony... I don't want to marry you.

TONY: *(Laughs)* Now don't talk silly.

CATHY: *(Screams)* I do not want to marry you.

A Silence

TONY: Come on Cath... What kind of joke do you call this?

CATHY: *(Softly)* No joke... No joke... I can't marry you... Not now... not ever.

TONY: *(Puts his arm around her)* Why not?

CATHY: *(Pulls away)* Don't touch me. Just don't touch me.

TONY: *(Loud)* Why not? Why not?

CATHY: Because I don't want to.... That's all.

TONY: *(Shouts, louder)* That's all? That's all? You don't want to?... I know who's behind all this. It's that friend of yours. Mis La-de-da Jean. Filling your head with feminist rubbish... Going to marry her are you?... Spending your honeymoon is Lesbos are you?....

CATHY: Leave her out of it. This has nothing to do with her. This is my decision.

TONY: *(Softly)* I'm sorry.... I didn't mean it... Come on Cath. You're just nervous, that's all. We love each other. Think of all the things we've planned together. This house. We're almost there. Our own little home.

CATHY: Your home! I hate this house, I'm never going to be here. Understand... I'm sorry... It's better I told you now than....

TONY: *(In fury)* Than when? When? Better than over two years ago when we met? Better than nine months ago when you dragged me into that Building Society to get this house wrapped around my neck? Better than having worked my butt off night and day to get it ready? Get it ready for what? Get it ready for you! You! You and me!

CATHY: I don't want to be tied down into a marriage.

TONY: Not so long ago, one of the things you said you wanted was to be married. Have a place of your own. Children. You spoke of nothing else.

CATHY: Well, I don't any more... I'm sorry.

TONY: Of course you don't. That friend of yours has made damned sure of that. Hasn't she?

CATHY: Jean has nothing to do with this... I just don't feel ready for marriage.

TONY: Okay. Okay. You don't feel ready for it. Okay. We'll cancel the wedding. We'll live together. Here.

CATHY: No.

TONY: Why not?

CATHY: It's the same as being married...

TONY: Okay. Okay. I'll live here. You carry on living at your Mum's.

CATHY: No.

TONY: So what you're really saying is, it's me. You want out from me?

CATHY: Yes... I'm afraid so.

TONY: But you said you loved me.

CATHY: I thought I did. I was wrong.

TONY: But dear Jean has convinced you you don't?

CATHY: No. Not Jean.

TONY: Who then?... Who then?

CATHY: Her... Her...brother.

TONY: Her brother?

CATHY: Yes... We've been seeing each other... I'm sorry.

TONY, shocked, stunned, unable to speak, clenches his fists, turns away from her.

TONY: *(Eventually)* You mean.... You mean... You and him... Have?...

CATHY: *(Softly)* Yes.... I love him and he...

He turns with raised fists, rushes towards her.

TONY: Get out! Get out! You bitch! Get out!

She quickly, in fear, moves to door, tries to speak. He moves towards her.

Get out of my house! Get out! Get out!

She exits. HEATHER nervously enters as he falls to his knees.

Cathy...Cathy... Cathy...

HEATHER moves to him. Reaches out to touch him. Hesitates. Withdraws. Sits on the easy chair. He slowly looks up.

HEATHER: *(Softly)* I'm sorry.

TONY: You... heard?

HEATHER: Yes... I'm afraid I...

TONY: How could she?

HEATHER: I don't know.

TONY: *(Hangs his head)* I feel like crying... but men don't do that, do they.

HEATHER: Perhaps they should. *(Pause)* Tea... would you?...

TONY: *(Emotional laugh)* Tea?... Tea.... Yes... Perhaps it... will...

HEATHER: Make you feel better?

TONY: Yes... something like that. *(HEATHER exits. He stands, replaces ply onto tea chest. Sits. Looks up at mantel)* What are we going to do now wallpaper? Looks like it's just you and me from now on.

HEATHER: *(Enters)* I've put sugar in. Do you...? *(Hands him a mug)*

TONY: Yes. Thank you. I got the posh cups out.

HEATHER: Oh you didn't need to do that, not for me... But thank you, it was a nice thought.

TONY: Not having many of those at the moment.

HEATHER: No. *(Sits)*

A silence.

TONY: Sorry about being so tactless about your... About your leg... I didn't...

HEATHER: Don't worry. How were you to know?

TONY: Felt awful... Feel awful.

HEATHER: Thank you for feeling awful. I appreciate sensitivity towards feelings. I like that quality... Is there anything I can do to...? To...?

TONY: Change the way I feel right now?

HEATHER: Yes.

TONY: No... I expect I haven't felt the half of it yet.

HEATHER: No... I'd better go. I'm sure you'd rather be alone.

TONY: No... Stay... Please.... I want you to... I couldn't handle the silence.

HEATHER: Perhaps silence is what you need.

TONY: We can be silent together.

HEATHER: If you want. Yes.

A silence.

TONY: Have you ever been... been hurt?

HEATHER: Yes. But not in the same context.

TONY: But been hurt?

HEATHER: By a relationship? No... I was badly upset when my Mother passed away.

TONY: Yes... I'm sorry. Your Dad told me.... So nobody has ever put you in this situation?... Walked out on you?

HEATHER: No.

TONY: Lucky you.

HEATHER: Nobody has ever walked in on me either.

TONY: Never had a....?

HEATHER: Boyfriend? No... Not really.

TONY: A lovely girl like you?

HEATHER: *(Embarrassed)* I am not lovely.

TONY: I disagree.

HEATHER: I don't feel lovely.... but then feelings are strange.... I watch other people, see the destruction they inflict upon each other with feelings... Sometimes I think it's better to be like me. Alone.

TONY: To be alone... Loneliness... I've never known that.

HEATHER: Then you're the lucky one, not me.

A silence.

TONY: Tell me about yourself.

HEATHER: I'm sure that's the last thing you want right now, listening to my boring lifestyle.

TONY: Let me be the judge of that. I want to hear. It may stop me thinking about murdering, you know who... So, what do you do with yourself? In the evenings? Weekends?

HEATHER: Nothing much. I watch tele, I read... And I spend a lot of time thinking.

TONY: Thinking? Thinking about what?

HEATHER: Stupid things really. Silly dreams. Things I would like. Things I know I shall never have...

TONY: Sometimes dreams come true.

HEATHER: Sometimes. Sometimes not.

TONY: *(Sadly)* No.

HEATHER: Sometimes I think I'm not here. *(He frowns)* It's as though I'm invisible... I have to pinch myself to see if I'm still alive.

TONY: I don't understand.

HEATHER: Forgive me... I'm just feeling sorry for myself.

TONY: *(Slipping into deep thought)* I know how you feel.

HEATHER: Yes... Sorry... *(Pause)* This morning I was sitting in the garden... I picked a daisy from the lawn. It may sound silly, but I felt so guilty I wanted to cry.... I only wanted to look at it closely... But to satisfy my curiosity the daisy, she had to die... I crushed her between my fingers to end her suffering.

TONY: *(Smiles weakly)* You're almost as daft as me.

HEATHER: I'm glad.

TONY: Would you mind if we swapped?

HEATHER: Swapped? Swapped what?

TONY: Seats... I'm whacked.

HEATHER: *(Stands)* Oh. Yes. Yes, of course... Look I'll go if you're tired.

TONY: *(Sits in chair)* Ah. That's better. No. Please. Stay. I like hearing you talk.

HEATHER: Would you mind if I fetched some cushions?

TONY: Why?

HEATHER: For me to sit on.

TONY: Yes if you want.

HEATHER: Won't be a moment or... Or would you rather come and watch the tele?... You'd be very welcome.

TONY: *(Softly)* No... no....

HEATHER: Shan't be a tick. *(Exits)*

TONY'S eyes are fixed firmly onto the mantel. The hand holding the mug falls to the side of the chair spilling the tea onto the floor.

TONY: *(Soft emotion)* A crushed daisy... With it's stem broken... Cath... Cath... Please... Come back.... Cath... I love you... I love... Please love me... *(Drops cup, puts hands over face)*

The surrounding lights begin to fade leaving only the chair and an area on the floor spotlighted.

HEATHER enters with cushions. She stops. Puts her fingers to her lips. Shows signs of inner compassion. She moves closer, places the cushions into the floor spotlight. Moves to him, her lips tremble, reaches out her hand to touch him, hesitates. Slowly sits on the cushions. Tears form in her eyes as the spotlights fade down to total blackout.

End of Scene 1

ACT I Scene 2

Almost midnight of the same day.

During the blackout HEATHER has changed places with TONY. The lights fade up to the two spotlights.

HEATHER is asleep in the chair. He hair has been let down. TONY is also asleep, sprawled across the floor. He wears a shirt that is unbuttoned to the waist, his shoes are off. In his hand an empty glass.

Standing on the tea chest an almost empty bottle of whisky. Beside the chair a half full glass. Scattered around are magazines, a photo album, several loose photographs and the remains of a Chinese take-away meal.

HEATHER awakes. Looks at her watch then at Tony. Picks up her glass and sips. She stands. Lowers herself down beside him. Touches his hair lightly. TONY makes the high-pitched mumble that finishes with a definite "Cath". She stands and goes back to the chair. She sits and begins to hum. The hum changes to soft singing.

HEATHER: *(Singing)*   I will comfort you,

Till the morning light.

You can call her name.

I don't mind. I don't mind.

If you're loving her,

I will understand.

I will play the game.

I don't mind. I don't mind.

Hearts are hurting now.
Words are burning now.
Like the shooting stars.
Can't quite reach them now.
Till it's far too late.
Yes it's far too late.
But I don't mind. I don't mind.

The door knocker rattles loudly. HEATHER stands and touches Tony with her foot.

HEATHER: Tony... Tony... Wake up.

He mumbles. A louder knock. Looking worried she moves to hall exit. The room lights fade up as she exits.

BILLY: *(Off)* Is my son here?

BILLY hurries in followed by Heather

HEATHER: I'm afraid he's asleep.

BILLY: *(Shaking Tony)* Tony. Wake up. Wake up. For God's sake, wake up. *(TONY mumbles. BILLY takes glass, smells it)* Been drinking has he? How much has he had?

HEATHER: Quite a lot, I'm afraid.

BILLY: *(Looks at the bottle)* So I see. *(Shakes him)* Tony, will you wake up. *(TONY mumbles repeatedly)* Listen to him will you. Just like his mother. Come on you. Will you wake up...

HEATHER: Mr Banks, I think you should know....

BILLY: I'll have to call his brother. Where's the nearest phone box, young lady?

HEATHER: You can use ours. Next door. Is something wrong? Can I help?

BILLY: I very much doubt it... His mother has disappeared. *(Kicks Tony)* Tony.

HEATHER: Disappeared? Where?

BILLY: She just wandered off... Tony... I wonder if you could do me a kindness Miss... Miss...?

HEATHER: Picture... Heather Picture... I live next door.

BILLY: Ah, I see, I'm Tony's father. *(Takes card from wallet)* I wonder, could you ring this number and ask to speak to Mr John Banks. Tell him to come here as soon as he can.... Tell him it's urgent.

HEATHER: John Banks? What if he asks why?

BILLY: Just tell him I want him here urgently.

HEATHER: Wouldn't it be better if you were to ring him yourself?

BILLY: No. I have to waken this drunken slob.... Now hurry along my dear.

HEATHER: *(Moves to exit)* Mr Banks... Tony's had rather an upset... So be gentle.

BILLY: I'll be gentle with him all right. *(To Tony)* Tony, will you please wake up.

HEATHER exits

TONY: Go away.

BILLY: *(Pulls him up)* Wake up damn you.

TONY: Get off will you... Oh. Oh, my head.

BILLY: Serve's you right.

TONY: Where's Heather?

BILLY: Gone next door to phone for your brother... And button your shirt... What on earth have you been playing at, young man?... I could have been Cath.

TONY: What are you on about?

BILLY: Middle of the night. Half naked. Sprawled all over the floor drinking with some innocent girl... I'm sure Cath would have been most impressed.

TONY: I don't give a toss what Cath thinks.

BILLY: Oh, I see. Now listen Tony, taking advantage with another woman is not the way to settle arguments.

TONY: Advantage? Advantage? What are you on about? I was just having a drink with a neighbour... And what are you doing here anyway?

BILLY: *(Picks up glass, pours a drink)* I shouldn't really, seeing as I'm driving, but I need it. *(Drinks)* It's your Mother. She's disappeared.

TONY: Disappeared?

BILLY: Yes. Wandered off.

TONY: Wandered off?

BILLY: Yes. She's not at home either.

TONY: Not at home?

BILLY: No... Will you stop repeating everything I say.

TONY: Look, Dad, please, I'm tipsy, Cathy's cleared off, my head's banging, I can't think straight, so, please, if you come to load my plate with even more worries, just sit down and tell me, one step at a time. Let me absorb it slowly.

BILLY: *(Sits on tea chest)* I'm worried Tony. She's wandered off before. I was getting quite used to it, but never at this hour of the night. Anything could happen to her. It's not safe on the streets at night.

TONY: No. Especially around the walkways.... How long has she been gone?

BILLY: Over two hours that I know of. It could be longer. I missed her around ten o'clock... And I'll have you know the walkways are perfectly safe.

TONY: Where have you looked?

BILLY: Everywhere.

TONY: Have you phoned the police?

BILLY: No, of course not, she's only been missing for a couple of hours... We were at the Town Hall, as you know. The last I saw of her was during Arnold Bunn's acceptance speech.

TONY: Arnold Bunn?

BILLY: Yes. Arnold Bunn.

TONY: Sorry Dad...

BILLY: The man's rich... Money talks... Anyhow, all is not lost. You are now looking at the deputy Lord Mayor.

TONY: Congratulations... Not what you wanted but...

BILLY: No. Well, there's always next year.... At the moment my only concern is to the whereabouts of your Mother. Where could she have got to? It was during Arnold's speech that she just stood up and left the room. Raised a few eyebrows, I can tell you. One does not go the Ladies during speeches... And I haven't seen her since.

TONY: You're sure you've checked everywhere?

BILLY: Of course.

TONY: And she didn't say where she was going or what she was going to do?

BILLY: No... You know what she's like. Her mind, it wanders... Arnold Bunn was cackling on about how things have changed in the city since he was a lad... She just stood up and walked out... I know he was spouting rubbish, but that was no excuse.

TONY: What sort of rubbish?

BILLY: It's of no importance.

TONY: Tell me. It may be relevant.

BILLY: Can't see how... He made some stupid joke about the brewery. How he would wait at the gate for his dad to bring out his wages on a Friday.

TONY: What brewery?

BILLY: The one that was in Barrack Street.

TONY: Barrack Street? Isn't that where you lived when you were first married? Did you go and look there?

BILLY: No. Why should she go to Barrack Street?

TONY: I don't know. But this morning she was on about it... upstairs... There's something wrong Dad... She's ill.

BILLY: It's just her age... Menopause problems... Yes. Just her age.

TONY: Dad, she's only fifty three!

HEATHER: *(Enters)* I'm sorry Mr Banks. His landlady said he was out.

BILLY: I'll bet he is... Probably snuggled up beside her between the sheets.... Landlady indeed.... How old is she?... Old enough to be his mother... It's a scandal.

TONY: Never mind about him... I think we should go down to Barrack Street.

BILLY: Perhaps you're right... Get your jacket... Four eyes are better than two.

TONY: It's upstairs... I think we'd better check back home. With luck she'll be tucked up in bed as well. *(Buttons shirt, searches room for shoes)* Shoes?... Shoes?

HEATHER: I'll get your jacket.... What room?

TONY: Thanks. Front. Your side.

She exits.

BILLY: What's wrong with the young lady's leg?

TONY: Polio.

BILLY: Oh... You haven't been...?

TONY: No Dad... Just a drink.

BILLY: Glad to hear it... It wouldn't be right... wedding only being three weeks away.

TONY: What wedding?

BILLY: Fight that big was it? Don't worry. I wouldn't mind having a pound for every time your Mother cancelled ours. She'll be back. All lovey-dovey. You're both tired that's all. All the work. The worry.

TONY: No Dad. It's off.... I'll tell you about it in the car. *(HEATHER enters without the jacket)* Couldn't you find it?

HEATHER: *(Concerned)* Yes, but... but... There was a woman in your bed. I think it may be your Mother.... She smiled and called me Jennifer.

MILLY enters. She seems to be in a trance and not hearing BILLY's ranting and raving as she sits in the easy chair.

BILLY: Where have you been woman? I've been looking everywhere for you. What on earth did you think you were playing at? Wandering off without a word? And during Arnold Bunn's speech. The looks people gave me. Do you realise, that for whatever reason you decided to leave, people looked upon it as sour grapes. Do you realise that? Do you?

TONY: Dad. Stop it... stop it.... She's ill....

BILLY: Too much to drink, that's her problem.

TONY: *(Kneels beside her)* Mum, it's Tony.

MILLY: *(Gazes around room)* Furniture.

BILLY: *(Loud)* Furniture?

TONY: Be quiet.... Where have you been Mum?

MILLY: It's under the stairs.

BILLY glares at her then turns away.

TONY: What is Mum?

MILLY: We need the money... Pennies... Sugar... Tea... Furniture... *(Waves hands in front of face brushing away invisible cobwebs)* Furniture... Jennifer... Who took them?

TONY: Mum, how did you get upstairs?

HEATHER: I'd left the door open when I went for the cushions. I locked it when you came back with the Chinese. I'm sorry.

TONY: Good thing you did. There's no knowing where she would have gone.

MILLY: *(Smiles)* Eat your biscuit, Jennifer.

TONY: Mum, who's Jennifer?

MILLY stares at him in disbelief, looks at Heather, frowns, puts hand to mouth, looks back at TONY in confusion.

MILLY: It's so green... So green.

TONY: Dad. Who's Jennifer?

BILLY: Oh, just some girl who lived in Barrack Street. *(Sharply)* Now stop this nonsense Milly.

TONY: Shut up Dad... She's ill.

MILLY: *(To Billy)* It's under the stairs.

BILLY: Under the stairs? What is she talking about?

MILLY: *(Upset)* I'll tell you.... I'll tell you... Furniture.... But I'll tell.... I must tell.... Under the stairs... It was... It was.... *(To Tony)* Tell him we need the money... For John... For John... John?... John?.... John?

TONY: That's it Mum. That's right. John. Who's John?

MILLY: He plays... He plays... Yes... Jennifer... We will.

TONY: Mum. Look at me. Who am I?

MILLY: I don't... I don't... John? John?

TONY: And who is that? *(Points at Billy)*

MILLY: Under the stairs. *(Distraught)* Under the stairs. Under the stairs. Under the stairs.

BILLY: *(Hissing)* Stop it. Stop it. Stop it.

TONY: Shut up.

A knock at the door

HEATHER: I'll go. *(Exits)*

BILLY: *(Calms, moves to Milly)* Milly?

MILLY: *(Snaps loudly)* Under the bloody stairs.

TONY: Dad, what's this about? What is she saying?

MILLY: *(Looks around room)* Did Jennifer eat her biscuit? *(To Tony)* Who are you?

TONY: I'm Tony. Your son. Who am I Mum?

Muffled voices are heard in the hall

BILLY: Milly... Mildred... Come on... Stop playing these silly games.

MILLY: *(Softly with venom)* Under the stairs.

HEATHER enters followed by SAM

HEATHER: It was my Dad... Perhaps he can help.

MILLY: We need the money.

SAM enters fully into room. He looks at Milly. Frowns. MILLY slowly looks up. She smiles.

TONY: Dad. Mr Picture is a nurse.

MILLY: *(Rising, stretching out arms to Sam. In total control)* Hello Sam.

STAGE BLACKS OUT

End of ACT I

ACT II Scene 1

Three weeks later. Friday 2.30pm.

The room is now furnished. Amongst the bits and pieces around the room there is a brass carriage clock. Hanging over the arm of a chair is a pair of black trousers. Beside the chair is a pair of black shoes. The opening action is performed in mime and to music.

(Suggest - "All Cried Out" by Jack Jones. From the Album "Harbour" APLI 0408 RCA)

HEATHER standing at an ironing board pressing a shirt. She now looks lovely. Her hair is down, she wears make-up, pale blue jeans and a large printed tee shirt belted at the waist with a curtain cord. The shirt ironed, she holds it up, smiles and kisses it lightly, moves to the chair and is about to drape it over the back when TONY comes rushing in.

TONY is wearing only underpants, a tee shirt and socks. His hair is a mess. She smiles, unconcerned at his lack of clothing, holds out shirt. TONY slips arms into sleeves, grabs trousers, pulls them on. Rushes out to the kitchen. HEATHER picks up shoes, "Huffs" onto the toes, polishes them on side of her jeans. TONY rushes in, sits, buttons shirt. HEATHER puts shoes on his feet. He holds out arms, she buttons sleeves. He stands up, picks up necktie, moves to mirror. HEATHER resumes ironing. TONY exits. Returns pulling on blazer. She moves to him. Puts a handkerchief into his pocket, straightens his tie, he combs his hair, she brushes his jacket.

TONY: *(Looking in mirror)* There, how do I look?

HEATHER: Very impressive. *(Returns to ironing board)*

TONY: You know Heather, I can't thank you enough for all you've done these past three weeks.

HEATHER: My pleasure.

TONY: Washing, ironing, cooking. I don't know what I would have done without you. But, you don't have to, you know.

HEATHER: Well, who's to do it then?

TONY: I suppose I'd have to cope on my own.

HEATHER: What's the point when I can do it?

TONY: Yes.

HEATHER: I like doing it... That's what friends are for.

TONY: Yes. But you've been more than that to me.

HEATHER: Have I?

TONY: Yes. My little soldier.

HEATHER: A soldier?

TONY: Yes. Picked me up when I was wounded.

HEATHER: Oh... And you're not now?

TONY: Yes. But not as much.... I live in hope.

HEATHER: If that's what you want.... But does Cath? I didn't think that was the reason she's asked you to meet her.

TONY: Yes I know, I know.

HEATHER: I gather that all she wants is to get her share of the pickings.

TONY: Or to make amends.

HEATHER: I'm glad for you.

TONY: No you're not... Now look Heather. I know you think I'm being silly rushing off to see her but...

HEATHER: Well, let's hope that she takes one look at you, bursts into tears and begs you to take her back.... You're a fool.

TONY: I love her.

HEATHER: Fools usually are in love.

TONY: God. You sound just like your Father.

HEATHER: Yes.

TONY: Look Heather, I know what you're thinking....

HEATHER: Do you?

TONY: I know you've done a lot for me. I would have gone crazy if you hadn't been here to hold my hand, and I know you are entitled to your opinion, but we all make mistakes. I'm sure Cathy wants to put her mistake right.

HEATHER: You think so?

TONY: Her wanting to get the house settled is just an excuse. I'm sure of it. She wants us to kiss and make up.

HEATHER: And you will?

TONY: Yes. Of course. That's what I want.

HEATHER: What are you going to do if all she does want is to get this house thing settled?... Come and ask me to hold your hand again? Not that I recall ever holding your hand.

TONY: I'm prepared for that outcome. But I've got this feeling... Just got this feeling... I'm sure you've had feelings about things before they happen.

HEATHER: Yes. But they never happen.

TONY: *(Looks at his watch)* Look, I have to go. I don't want to be late. Cath hates to be kept waiting... How do I look?

HEATHER: *(Shakes her head, smiles)* You look lovely.

TONY: *(Moves to exit)* I'll leave you to lock up... Wish me luck. *(Exits)*

HEATHER: *(Softly)* Yes. Good luck Tony... Good luck. *(Slams iron down onto shirt, works in anger. Stops suddenly, puts iron aside, picks up shirt, crumples it, tosses it into basket)* And no luck for Heather. *(Exits to the kitchen)*

SAM enters.

SAM: Heather... You about?... Heather love.

HEATHER: *(Enters)* Hello Dad. *(Kisses him)* Want a cuppa?

SAM: No. I want to get to my bed. It's been a long night. I just came to find where you were and to tell you not to go pushing the hoover or anything. I need a good day's sleep. *(Moves to exit)* These nights will be the death of me. *(Turns)* Will you be staying here much longer?

HEATHER: Just got to finish the ironing.

SAM: You haven't got to do anything. You can do it, yes. But not got to.

HEATHER: I know that. But I like doing it.

SAM: Yes, but why?

HEATHER: I just do... I do it for you.

SAM: I'm different. I'm family... Who's Tony? I ask myself.

HEATHER: I don't understand.

SAM: What's he to you?

HEATHER: A friend.

SAM: No more than a friend?

HEATHER: No... Don't be silly.

SAM: You sure of that?

HEATHER: Of course I'm sure... He wants her... not me.

SAM: But you'd like him to?

HEATHER: No.

SAM: Come on love. I've been around far too long not to recognise the old twinkle in the eyes.

HEATHER: My eyes are not twinkling.

SAM: Granted not now. Only when he's in the same room as you. Or when you're sitting quietly with thoughts, those thoughts written all over your face, then they twinkle... But be careful love. Daydreams are fine, but reality can sometimes be very painful... Where is he, by the way?

HEATHER: Gone to meet Cath... She snapped her fingers and he went running... He's hoping to patch things up. And I don't give a damn if they do, so that puts paid to your speculations.

SAM: Does it?

HEATHER: Yes. And a fine day she picked if you ask me. They were supposed to be walking down the aisle tomorrow... But he seems to have forgotten... If you want to see twinkling eyes then you should get a look at his... He went rushing out. Tarted up to the eyeballs... He's a fool.... He deserves whatever he gets... If he gets it that is.

SAM: Be careful love. *(Exits, speaking)* Your eyes have started to twinkle again.

HEATHER: *(Loud)* Rubbish. *(Moves to mirror)* They are not twinkling. *(Softly)* They are not twinkling... *(Exits to kitchen)*

Mumbling voices from hall. Two men and Cathy.

CATHY: *(Off)* Front bedroom. Everything but his clothes... That corner unit on the stairs is mine as well. *(Mumbling)* Pass it here then. I'll take it if it's in your way... And hurry.

Silence

HEATHER enters with a mug of tea. Resumes ironing. A bump heard from upstairs. She looks up.

HEATHER: Don't be so noisy Dad. *(More bumping)* What's he doing?

The next bump is definitely from above. She looks worried. Freezes. Looks slowly to ceiling. CATHY enters carrying a suitcase. She is taken aback by the sight of Heather. She puts the case down.

CATHY: Oh... Who might you be then?

HEATHER: What's... What's going... on?

CATHY: I said, "Who are you?"

HEATHER: I'm a friend of Tony's... What's going on?

CATHY: This is not your business. And if you're refusing to tell me who you are I suggest you get out of my house.

HEATHER: What's happening?

CATHY: Will you please leave so that I can get on with what I came here to do.

HEATHER: This is Tony's house.

CATHY: Not all of it... *(Opens suitcase, begins packing small items)*

HEATHER: What are you doing? You can't do that.

CATHY: Want to bet... And who the hell are you to say what I can and can't do... I told you to get out of my house and I meant it.

HEATHER: *(Firmly)* I'm a friend of Tony's and I'll only leave at his say so.

CATHY: God. He didn't waste much time, did he.

HEATHER: He's a free agent. At least he waited until... Until... More than you can say.

CATHY: As far as I'm concerned, I don't give a monkey's what he does or who he does it with. Sleeping with him are you?... Not much good in bed, is he!

HEATHER: I wouldn't know....

CATHY: *(Laughs)* Exactly. That's what I mean.

HEATHER: *(Angry)* I demand to know what you think you're doing.

CATHY: *(Ignores her. Takes clock)* This is mine... And you are no one to demand anything. Apart from some slut he's picked up with.

HEATHER: How dare you call me that? You of all people, after you...

CATHY: Easy... *(Picks up mug of tea)* One night stand, are you? Got you doing the ironing, has he? Good at getting others to skimp for him... But... Was it worth it, love? *(Empties tea into basket. Holds up mug)* This is mine too.

HEATHER: *(Horror struck)* Look what you've done... His shirt... his best shirt..

CATHY: Good... Teach him not to use my things. *(Exits to kitchen)*

HEATHER moves quickly to the exit. Exits.

HEATHER: *(off)* You can't do this.

MAN'S VOICE: *(Off)* Better see the lady in there, love. We're only doing what we're told.

HEATHER backs into room.

HEATHER: *(Softly)* She can't do this... She can't. *(Moves quickly to telephone. Dials)* Come on... come on.... Wake up Dad... wake up.

CATHY enters carrying several kitchen items. Throws them into case. Moves quickly to Heather. Grabs her by the hair and pulls her away from the phone, knocks her to the floor, replaces receiver.

CATHY: Now look you, I don't know who you are and I don't honestly give a damn, but keep out of this... I'm taking what's rightfully mine. Nothing else. If you're so concerned for that 'toe rag' then you can stay and keep check exactly what I take. I expect you've had your grubby hands on everything that's his, and as we both know, he hasn't got a lot. These things are mine. *(HEATHER pulls herself up, moves to the kitchen exit)* And I'm not having some cheap scrubber... Hello... What's he been up to?... Kicked you in the leg did he?.... In his sleep?

HEATHER: *(Stops sharply. Breathes in deeply)* Now look here you... I do not have to put up with your cheap remarks. You disgust me.

CATHY: Good. I hope you'll be happy living here... with him. God help you.

HEATHER: I do not live here... I live next door and...

CATHY: That's handy.

HEATHER: Tony is just a friend... I've been helping him...

CATHY: I'll bet you have.

HEATHER: After what you did...

CATHY: Mind your own business and get next door where you belong. I'm sure you've got lots to do... Polish your red light perhaps?... You wouldn't happen to be a friend of his brother's too, would you?*(Laughs)*

HEATHER: *(Moves to the ironing board, picks up the iron)* That's it. I'm staying. Staying until he comes back... My God, what kind of person are you?... He's gone to meet you, fool that he is, and do you know what he's hoping for?

CATHY: No. But I expect you're dying to tell me.

HEATHER: You ought to hate yourself for what you've done.

CATHY: I quite enjoy hating myself actually.

HEATHER: And he loves you.

CATHY: And I hate the idea that he loves me.

HEATHER: He's hoping that you might have changed your mind. Hoping that you might come back to him. He loves you... God knows why.

CATHY: Tough old world, isn't it. *(Grabs iron)* This is mine too. *(HEATHER does not give up the iron willingly)* Give it to me, you cow, before I give you a limp in your other leg. *(She wins the fight)* Right. Thank you. *(Exits to hall. Off)* Put this at the front... Mind, it's still hot... Are you sure you've got everything?... Right... I'll be there in a tick. *(Returns into room, closes case)* When he gets back you can tell him I've taken what's mine... If there's anything else, he can keep it... Apart from the oven... The gas board will be here on Monday to disconnect it. And my two friends, my two very large friends, will be here on Tuesday to pick it up... I'd advise him to be out if I were him... Oh, and by the way, that curtain cord you're wearing is mine... But I give it to you as a gift... along with him... You're welcome to them both. *(Exits)*

HEATHER: *(Pressing onto ironing board)* How can you love her?... How can you? *(Moves to telephone)* I must let you know. *(Picks up telephone directory, finds number, dials...)* Come on... Come on.... Answer... Ah, good afternoon. I was wondering if a Mr Tony Banks has arrived there yet?... Yes. Tony Banks... Yes he does have an account... Well has he been in?... Yes, he had an appointment... No. I don't know who with... He was meeting his future wife there... I don't know. Cathy something or other... He may be waiting outside. I was wondering if you could possibly?... It is very urgent... You don't understand. I have to talk to him... Yes. I told you. He's supposed to be meeting her there and she... *(Puts her hand over mouthpiece)* Of course. Of course. How could I be so stupid? *(She speaks into phone)* Look, if he comes in, would you tell him to ring home immediately? It is very urgent. Yes. No. Thank you. Goodbye. *(Hangs up)* My God, how on earth do these people manage to keep their jobs... *(Picks up shirt)* Better get this washed before he gets back... Stupid bitch... *(Exits to kitchen)*

MILLY enters

MILLY: Tony... Are you there love?... It's your Mum.

HEATHER: *(Enters)* Hello Mrs Banks... I'm afraid Tony's had to go out.

MILLY: Oh... Who are you?... I seem to know you from somewhere, but I can't think where.

HEATHER: Heather. We have met a few times before. I've been helping since... Since...

MILLY: Oh yes, of course... Heather?.... I always think of you as a Jennifer. The rooms's looking nice.

HEATHER: It was until.... I've asked Tony to ring... Cathy was here. She's only just left... She took all her things... Even the bed.

MILLY: I saw a van pulling away... Was that her? Wish I'd been here. Treating the poor boy like that. And with only three months to go. Took the bed did she? Looks as though he'll have to come home and live with us again. I didn't like the idea in the first place. Him living here alone. Not after... too lonely... Do you like this? *(Takes a package out of her shopping bag)* It's a new clock for the mantel. I never did... Oh. Where's it gone?

HEATHER: She took that as well. Said it was hers.

MILLY: But it's not hers. I bought her that for her birthday. Belongs to them both... Well never mind. It was far too small... Is there a cup of tea going by any chance, love? I'm parched.

HEATHER: No. But I'll make you one... Is Mr Banks not with you?

MILLY: No. I left him up the city. He went to the Town Hall. Had to get some papers or something. I didn't want to go. My feet are killing me. I grabbed a taxi and told him I'd meet him here. Mind you, knowing him, he'll be hours yet...Think I'll sit and put my feet up.

HEATHER: Yes. I'll make some tea. Shan't be a tick.

MILLY: *(Sits, puts feet up on stool)* That's a good girl... Pity our Tony didn't find himself someone like you in the first place.

HEATHER: Tea! *(Exits)*

MILLY: *(Calls through)* You know, Jennifer, I love this little house. Cosy. I like cosy rooms... I'd love a house like this... Living in a big house is terrible... Some wouldn't understand that... It's all very well to create an impression, but when the doors are shut and the curtains are drawn, it's still like living in a museum... As for possessions, who needs them? *(Stands, walks around. During the following speech she begins to regress and become confused)* Possessions... I had real possessions once... Now all I have are valuable items... Investments... Works of art... Ugly things... He has odd tastes... Never mind what it looks like, just as long as it increases in value... Well what about my china dancing ladies... Mother bought me them... Yarmouth Market. Bank holiday... *(Closes eyes)* No... Don't Mother... You couldn't possibly afford them... I want you to have them... When I'm dead and gone... Don't die... Don't die... *(Opens eyes)* China dancing ladies... In the bin... "Didn't suit", he said... "Must throw away Barrack Street", he said.... "Not in that class any more, Mildred", he said.... "People who live on Newmarket Road do not have Yarmouth Market junk sitting on their sideboard"... Not with me now Mother... Gone... I lost you... Lost my home for a house... Friends for cheese and wine... Lost... Gone... Children gone... Billy?... Didn't lose him... Never really had him to lose I suppose... You told me... "Selfish", you said... *(Begins to hum "My Mother's Eyes")* Jennifer, do you like my ladies?... Under the stairs my dear... Yes... Only one... Don't want you getting fatter... My. My aren't we getting to be the cubby one... Too many biscuits... Under the stairs... Yes... Too many biscuits. *(Her voice begins to raise as she becomes confused)* Not true... Not true... Jennifer?.... My Jennifer?... Don't... Don't run Jennifer... Don't run... Don't run.... *(She becomes silent. Sits slowly onto the sofa. Her fingers twist nervously together. Speaks slowly and softly)* Yes dear... We will... Uncle Billy and me... Uncle Billy loves you... Our own child Jennifer... We'll look after you... *(Shouts)* I found it under the bloody stairs, Billy. *(She falls into a deep silence)*

SAM enters wearing pyjamas and a dressing room

SAM: Hello Milly. *(No response from Milly)* Is Heather around? *(No response)* Are you all right, Milly? *(No response)* If you want to talk, Milly... You know... *(Heather enters with mugs of tea)*

HEATHER: Hello, Dad. Couldn't you sleep?

SAM: No... What's been happening here?

HEATHER: His girlfriend came and took all her things... I couldn't stop them.

SAM: Was Mrs Banks here?

HEATHER: No. Your tea Mrs Banks. *(No response)*

SAM: How long has she been like this?

HEATHER: ...But... I only just went to make tea, she was.... What's happened?... Tea, Mrs Banks? *(No response. MILLY stands and moves to mantel)*

MILLY: *(Softly)* I want to go back... I want to go back.

SAM: Back where Milly?

MILLY: To my home... To my home... I was happy there.

HEATHER: Dad will run you in the car if that's what you want... But drink your tea first...

MILLY: I was happy in Barrack Street.

BILLY enters with great excitement.

BILLY: Milly. Milly. I have some wonderful news. *(Dances her about the room)* Wonderful. Wonderful news. Arnold Bunn has had a heart attack.

MILLY stares into space, horrified. BILLY moves away from her. During his next speech MILLY moves to the kitchen exit and exits unnoticed.

BILLY: I only popped in to pick up some papers. I bumped into John Samson in the reception. "Heard about poor Arnold?" he said. "No", I said. "In intensive care... Keeled over last night during a Women's Institute dinner". Funny thing about it was he was talking about the National Health at the time... It's wonderful. God. Do you realise what this means, Milly?... I am now the... Milly?... Milly?... Where is she?

HEATHER: She was there just a moment...

BILLY: *(Calling)* Milly! Milly!

HEATHER: She must have gone into the kitchen. *(Exits)*

SAM: Congratulations... Mr Banks... Not the best way to get...

BILLY: He should never have been elected in the first place. Everyone said it should have been me... And now it's...

HEATHER: *(Enters)* She's not there. The back door was wide open and so was the gate... She's gone.

BILLY: Stupid woman... I'm getting to the end of my tether with her, I can tell you. Any other woman would have been delighted...

SAM: Mr Banks... Your wife is not well.

BILLY: Nonsense... Just getting old and senile.

SAM: And isn't senility an illness, Mr Banks?

BILLY: You know what I mean... She does it to draw attention to herself.

HEATHER: She was not at all well Mr Banks... She was most strange.

BILLY: She wanders... In her mind and in her feet... She'll be back.

HEATHER: She was on about Barrack Street.

BILLY: Oh, Barrack Street... Yes, her favourite subject. We lived in no more than a slum shack down there. Now she has one of the finest houses in the city and she pines for that dump... Never been able to figure women out... Do you have anything like this to put up with, Mr... Mr...Er...

SAM: Picture... But call me Sam. No, Mr Banks, I do not... Maybe it's because I'm not the same person as you.

BILLY: Well, you're a lucky man... To me, women have only one purpose in life and that is to drive men out of their minds.

HEATHER: I do think we should try to find her.

BILLY: Don't worry my dear. She'll come back... She always does.

HEATHER: But I think...

BILLY: You'll spend all day and not find her... Norwich is a big place, my dear... I've had to deal with this several times, I can tell you... It's better to sit tight and let her make her own way back.

SAM: Heather... Go to Barrack Street... Behind where the brewery used to be there's a sloping green. Know where I mean?

HEATHER: Yes, but....

SAM: Take my car... At the left of the green you'll find a secluded area surrounded by gorse... Milly will be there... Tell her Sam wants to talk to her.

HEATHER: But...

SAM: Do as I say... Now hurry...

BILLY: Tell her I want a few words with her too... No. Never mind about driving, I'll go. *(Turns on Sam)* How do you know she'll be there?

SAM: I just do... And I don't think you should go Mr Banks... Heather knows how to deal with this kind of thing.

BILLY: But she's... She's my wife.

SAM: Please do as I say. Leave it to Heather... Now run along love. My car keys are hanging in the hall.

HEATHER exits. A silence.

BILLY: Stupid woman. Causing everyone all this worry.... May as well drink this tea. *(Picks up mug, sips)* Ugh... Sugar. *(Picks up second mug)* Ah. That's better... Do you take sugar?

SAM: Yes.

BILLY: Cup of tea there if you want one.

SAM: Not just yet.

BILLY: Suit yourself... If she's not back in half an hour...

SAM: She'll be back...

BILLY: Tell me. What makes you think she'd go to Barrack Street?

SAM: Lots of memories there for her.

BILLY: I have memories of Barrack Street. Not all good ones mind. Mostly bad. But I don't go running back there every five minutes.

SAM: And what about the people? Fond memories of them?

BILLY: One or two. Yes. Why do you ask?

SAM: Ever wondered what Jennifer would be doing if...

BILLY: What do you know about Jennifer?

SAM: She lived next door to you.

BILLY: *(Concerned)* Yes.

SAM: Life was not good for Jennifer. Perhaps it was better she...

BILLY: Yes... Most unfortunate.

SAM: Her Father killed himself, did you know?

BILLY: Yes.

SAM: Must have been hard to live with that... I expect it would make one feel like a failure.

BILLY: Yes I suppose you're... Yes, I never thought of it like that.

SAM: Shortly after, her Mother died of a broken heart... Did you know that?

BILLY: I knew she died. Yes. But I didn't know what of.

SAM: Perhaps she felt failure too.

BILLY: Possibly. I wouldn't know.

SAM: What about you failing Jennifer?

BILLY: Pardon?

SAM: You can't bear that word, can you Billy... Failure.

BILLY: Now look. I don't know what you're driving at. Jennifer Goodson lost her father and then her mother, all in a short space of time... She was an orphan... But she was luckier than most orphans... She had her Aunt to look after her. Not some wretched institution.

SAM: Wasn't it more her looking after the Aunt? The invalid Aunt?

BILLY: True. True. But we helped the girl as much as we could... Money was scarce... Milly would give the poor girl biscuits if we had them in the house...

SAM: *(Slowly)* So. You gave Jennifer a biscuit... And Jennifer gave you a big house up on Newmarket Road...

BILLY: What?

SAM: A good job... Flash car... Money in the bank... What more could one ask in return for a biscuit.

BILLY: I'm beginning to think you're as crazy as my wife.

SAM: Crazy? Perhaps I am... Crazy enough to know that when you moved to Barrack Street you were no more than an ambitious shop steward in the building trade... A common bricklayer...

BILLY: Yes. I was a bricklayer... And a Union representative.... So?

SAM: And very active in the Socialist Party?

BILLY: Yes... What has this to do with Jennifer?

SAM: Not Jennifer... Jennifer's Uncle... Her Mother's brother... He would visit his other sister quite often down in Barrack Street. Very generous he was too, to his poor half blind, deaf sister, caring for the orphaned niece... And very generous to you also, wasn't he...? Poor little Jennifer... So wanting to talk...

So she spoke to the kind man who's wife gave her biscuits...

BILLY: *(Horrified)* How on earth?..

SAM: Milly told me...

BILLY: Milly told you?... Milly told you?... But it was years before she knew... And why should she tell you?... You were nothing but the...

SAM: All a part of the job, Billy...

BILLY: You don't know anything... You have nothing on me.

SAM: Can't say I want anything on you, Mr Banks. You or her Mother's brother... A man of influence... A very public figure... A scandal would have been out of the question.

BILLY: *(Sits. Softly)* The man was an animal... She was just a child... *(Loud)* I made damned sure he paid for it. Damned sure... A filthy animal.

SAM: Isn't that blackmail, Billy?...

BILLY: I did not blackmail anyone... I suggest you be very careful what you say... You have no proof... None whatsoever.

SAM: No. That's true... Only Milly's memories.

BILLY: And we all know how reliable they are... And I also suggest you know very little.

SAM: True. I expect I don't know the half of it... But then what do I know?... You moved into Barrack Street after you married Milly... Lots to be done in the house, wasn't there, Billy?... Just like young Tony, at it night and day.

BILLY: I do not need you to give me an account of my life, thank you.

SAM: I believe you were upstairs decorating the back bedroom when you first heard the noises coming through the wall... A man and a young girl... A very young girl... You became suspicious right from that moment. Am I right, Billy?

BILLY: Yes... But I couldn't be sure... I dismissed it.

SAM: Until you saw the man. And lo and behold you recognised him... A very important man indeed... Very influential... The kind of friend you needed... You being so ambitious.

BILLY: How dare you. I told you, I had no proof.

SAM: And the noises continued?

BILLY: Yes... You seem to know they did.

SAM: But you had to make sure. And when you were, you kept it to yourself, you never told anyone. Not even Milly.

BILLY: I had no proof.

SAM: And you had your reasons. Not even Milly?... The next step was to encourage Jennifer into your house, knowing Milly would be sympathetic towards her?

BILLY: And why not?... The poor kid was having a lousy time looking after that Aunt... And also contending with what I suspected... What would you have done?

SAM: Told the wife, I think... Yes, I'm sure I would. Women are better at handling these things than men... And I would have been concerned for the girl's welfare.

BILLY: So was I.

SAM: Oh no. You were only concerned about your own welfare Billy... But you needed evidence.

BILLY: Yes... It's a very serious accusation...

SAM: So you befriended Jennifer. Knowing what you did, and you being such a lovable man, it was easy to manipulate conversations to make her feel she could trust you.

BILLY: No... That is not true.

SAM: Very keen photographer was Uncle, wasn't he? Had a darkroom next door. One of the reasons he visited so often, wasn't it?

BILLY: Yes... I still insist that what I did was for the best. Well, at the time, I thought it was... I should have gone straight to the police... I realise that now... You can always think of things you should have done after it's happened... Then it's too late.

SAM: Yes. Perhaps it wasn't wise for you to become her Uncle Billy... A man she could trust... To turn to for help... But you needed proof, didn't you Billy?... You couldn't help her unless you had proof... "Anything Jennifer. Anything". Isn't that what you kept saying?... "I can't help you unless"... Then during one of your cosy discussions she told you about the photographs... "Now if I could lay my hands on one of those, Jennifer"... And you kept telling her that, didn't you?

BILLY: You have no idea what it was like to sit and hear an innocent child speak of such things.

SAM: Haven't I?... Somehow or other, and God knows how, Jennifer managed to get a key to the darkroom... Knew a bit about photography yourself, didn't you Uncle Billy.... Took the film out of the camera and developed the proof you so badly needed.

BILLY: Yes. Damn you, yes... I thought I was going to be sick. The man was nothing more than....

SAM: A subject for blackmail?

BILLY: No.

SAM: Oh yes. Suddenly Billy Bank's name was on everyone's lips. A common bricklayer who threw away his trowel and became a building contractor, never to dirty his hands again. A successful business man suddenly elevated up through the corridors of political power... The man with all the ideals and ideas to promote equality for all... Justice for all... But what about justice for Jennifer!

BILLY: He never touched her again... I made sure of that... I kept my promise... That's all she wanted.

SAM: After over a year of waiting, yes, Jennifer finally got what she wanted. But what did you want Billy?

BILLY: I've worked for all I have. Worked hard... And you have no right to say different.

SAM: No, perhaps I haven't. But it didn't finish there did it Billy?... Jennifer came to you again with a bigger problem... She was with child... You really had Uncle by the short and curly's then, didn't you?

BILLY: I was protecting her. Can't you see that?

SAM: The only protection you gave was to him and your future prosperity... It's amazing how vulnerable that child was to your manipulation. "You must never tell who the father is Jennifer... Not in your interest, or the baby's... Me and Milly would look after you... Help you".... What with Billy? Money!... She hid it well. Seven and a half months gone before Milly noticed. Noticed it was more than chubbiness... Pity Milly was so late in knowing... Pity she was so judgemental on the girl... Scolding her... Poor kid... Poor Jennifer... Couldn't handle Milly's chastisement... Ran out... Onto the road... Bang... Sat and held her hand as she gave birth, didn't you Billy... Held her hand until she died.... The last words that child heard was you saying... "We'll take care of it Jennifer. We'll take care of it"... Well you certainly knew how to take care of things... Didn't you?

BILLY: *(Softly)* And Milly told you all this?

SAM: Yes.... Over coffee.... Ground coffee... Poured from a silver coffeepot into a bone chine teacup on a silver tray over a solid oak table in the kitchen of a five bedroom house on Newmarket Road... Out in the garden was a little boy of five or six playing with his new electric car... John... Jennifer's son...

BILLY: We adopted the boy because we promised... It was not easy.

SAM: And the money kept rolling in.

BILLY: No.

SAM: Yes... Rolling in until Milly, looking for memories of Barrack Street in the cellar under the stairs found your little package... Your little gold mine... It was then that your days of blackmailing came to an end... Just think... If he were still alive and you still had access to your gold mine... You could have been Lord Mayor years ago...

BILLY: *(Puts his head in his hands)* How could she betray me... How could she? My wife talking to a stranger.

SAM: Betray?... That's a strong word Billy, my boy. Milly was like Jennifer. She needed someone to talk to.

BILLY: How long have you known all this?

SAM: Years.

BILLY: And you did nothing about it?

SAM: No point... Jenny's gone... It's over.

BILLY: *(Very sadly)* Yes, you're right... It's over...These things happen... I lay awake at night thinking how wrongly I handled the whole affair... You say blackmail... I suppose it was... At the time I thought it was an act of courage.

SAM: Courage?

BILLY: As you said, he was a very important person. I was just a bricklayer, a good bricklayer. I took a pride in my work. And, I'll have you know, my business was built from sweat and hard work, not from what you are implying. I went to his office. Threw his filth at him. I made him swear he was never to visit that house again... Or else... What more could I have done?

SAM: Don't ask me to judge you... I leave that to your conscience and God... and Milly's memories. *(Turns away, pauses, sings softly)* Poor Jenny is a weeping, A weeping, a weeping, Poor Jenny is a weeping. On a bright summer's day. On the grass we all must lay. Stand up and choose the one you love.

During the song TONY enters. His head is down. He throws off his jacket. Sits. Looks up.

TONY: Hello Dad... God. What's happened? *(Jumps up)* Where are my things?

SAM: Cathy's been here... Took what she said was hers.

TONY: What!

BILLY: Good Lord... When did this happen?

SAM: Just before you arrived... Sorry Tony. Heather tried to contact you.

TONY: Heather? Heather? She let that cow take my things?

SAM: Calm down son. She only took what was hers. Heather tried to stop them.

TONY: Them?

SAM: She had two men with her. They took your bed, I'm afraid.

TONY: Took my bed? Took my bed? *(Rushes out)* I'll kill her... I'll kill her.

BILLY: The nerve of that one is beyond belief. Mind you, can't say I'm surprised. The moment I first set eyes on that girl I knew she would be trouble... She's a member of the Conservative Party. What can you expect.

SAM: So am I.

BILLY: Oh.

TONY: *(Rushes in)* She'll not get away with this. Mark my words. She'll not get away with it. *(Grabs phone, dials furiously)* There was me thinking she was sorry... A trick. A bloody trick to get me out of the house... Hello... Is your bloody daughter there?... Don't give me that... She's there. I know she is.... Tell that cow to get off her arse and.... Hello.... Hello.... Don't you hang up on me, you bitch. *(Re-dials)* I don't care how big you are mate... Do you know what she's done? Do you?.... Broke into my house. Stole my furniture... My furniture mate... When she walked out she lost all claim to... I don't give a

damn what the bloody Citizen's Advice Bureau told her... It's my stuff and
I'm.... *(Slams phone down, re-dials)* Put that phone back on the hook. *(Slams
phone down)* They're not getting away with it. Over my dead body.

BILLY: Calm down son... All this anger will get you nowhere.

SAM: Your father's right, Tony. What you need to do is sit down and work out
what's missing. What's hers and what's....

TONY: *(Shouting)* Nothing is hers. Nothing. *(Grabs jacket)* It's mine. Mine...
and she's not having it. *(Rushes out)*

BILLY: *(Stands)* Tony... Tony... Don't be such a fool. Come back. Use a bit of
sense. *(Exits briefly, then returns)* He's gone off like a mad thing... I'd better
follow him. Mind you, the way he drives he's already half way over the city...
Think I'd better warn her parents. *(Goes to phone, searches for number in
directory)* Kids today, Sam. What are we to do with them? Didn't know each
other more than five minutes before they were planning to be wed. *(Dials)*
Mortgage round their necks. He's got more to worry about than a few bits and
pieces, I can tell you... Engaged... Still off the hook... Oh well. On their heads
be it... *(Replaces receiver)*

HEATHER enters, MILLY clinging to her arm in a trance-like state.

HEATHER: There we are Mrs Banks. All safe and sound. *(Leads her to a
chair)* Now sit yourself down and I'll make us all a nice cup of tea.

BILLY: *(False concern)* Milly, they tell me you've not been feeling too good.

MILLY: *(Ignoring him)* Not green any more...

BILLY: *(Kneels beside her)* What's not green dear?

MILLY: Grass... Grass was green... *(Looks at Sam)* Did you make it green?...
No... Where is it?

BILLY: I don't understand this... It's almost as if she doesn't know us.

HEATHER: She's been like this ever since I found her.

SAM: Was she where I said, love?

HEATHER: Yes. She was sitting on a log... Singing.

BILLY: Singing?

HEATHER: Yes. Poor Jenny is a weeping.

BILLY stands, turns away

SAM: Go make that tea, love.

HEATHER exits, after giving a concerned look at MILLY.

SAM: We just can't get rid of Jennifer can we Billy.

MILLY: I... I've been there... It was green... I'm sure it was... I wanted it to be.

SAM: It was Milly... Very green... Look at me Milly... Who am I?... Do you know?... Say my name.

She struggles with her mind. Waves hands in front of face.

MILLY: All over it was... I'm sure... Could it?... Why did it?... You can see all of it now... So wide... So wide... All over it was... Poor Jenny is a weeping.

SAM: Billy, find me some paper and something to write with.

BILLY: Paper? What for?

SAM: Just find me some. Look in the drawer... I want to try something.

BILLY begins to search

MILLY: Little squares... on a nail...

SAM: Milly.

MILLY: *(Smiles)* News of the World.

SAM: Yes... What have you read in the News of the World? Who is the Prime Minister, Milly?.... What's her name?

MILLY: *(Waving hands)* Win... Win... Church... Winchurch.

SAM: *(Gently takes her hands)* What's your name?.... Think.... Who are you?

She struggles against his grip. BILLY moves to them with paper and a pencil.

BILLY: I've never seen her this bad before...

SAM: Perhaps you didn't look... Milly... this is your husband. Tell him what his name is...

She continues to struggle.

BILLY: Billy love... It's Billy.

SAM: Milly. Say it. Billy. William. Your husband. Say it. Say Billy.

MILLY: B...Bi... Billiffer...

SAM: Tell us the names of your children Milly.

MILLY: *(Loud)* John? John?.. John?

SAM releases her and takes the pencil and paper. Writes the number one hundred in large numerals. Holds it up for her to see.

SAM: See this Milly?... One hundred... What is it?

MILLY: One... Hund...dred...

SAM: Good... Now... One hundred take away seven.

MILLY: *(Sharply)* Ninety three.

SAM: Ninety three take away seven.

MILLY: Eighty six.

SAM: Take away seven.

MILLY: Seventy nine.

SAM: Take away seven.

MILLY: Ninety... Seven... Seventy... Nine... Seven... Sixty... Ninety seven... Sixty...

SAM: Now Milly, I want you to do something for me. Will you do that?

MILLY: *(Nodding)* Seventy nine... Seven.... Ninety....

SAM: I want you to draw me a circle. *(Places paper onto her lap, puts pencil into her hand)* A circle Milly... Show me... How do we draw a circle?

She places pencil onto paper. Holds pencil still. Looks deeply confused. She looks up, shakes her head.

SAM: Draw me a circle Milly. *(She looks at paper then at him.)* A square then... Try a square... Like the News of the World.

She begins to tremble. She slowly pushed the pencil across the paper drawing a jagged line. It moves off the paper. She drops it to the floor.

MILLY: It was green... Red... Red makes it brown... Not green... *(Slowly covers eyes with hands.)* Sleep... Sleep...

Sam stands. Billy is distressed.

SAM: She needs a doctor Billy... A good doctor.

BILLY: I'll get her home... Get Ellis in... Oh well, we'll get her into a good nursing home. I can afford it. It probably won't be for long anyway.

SAM: Get her to a doctor... The mind is a strange thing... Whatever it is the doctor will explain, I don 't want to put false worries into your head... You've got a lot of caring to do... Caring for somebody else instead of yourself... It'll take a lot of getting used to...

BILLY: Help me get her into the car . . . . I'll get her home to bed and get Ellis in straight away... He's a friend of mine... Play the occasional round of golf together...

They raise Milly out of the chair and move to the exit.

SAM: You '11 have no time for rounds of golf Mr Banks... Or prancing around as the Lord Mayor either...

They exit.

HEATHER: *(Enters with tea tray.)* Oh . Where is everybody?

(Places tray onto coffee table. Moves to window.) Goodbye Mrs Banks... I hope you'll soon feel better... Hope you find your patch of green grass again. *(Moves back into room, sits.)*

SAM: *(Enters)* Sorry about the tea love but it was best he gets her home.

HEATHER: Is Mrs Banks going to be all right?

SAM: *(Sits)* No love , I don't think she is.

HEATHER: It was most strange. When I found her she was sitting singing that song. She said she was looking for a patch of green grass... She was surrounded by grass.

SAM: It was a special patch love... She's been looking for it ever since they widened Barrack Street.

HEATHER: I don't understand?

SAM: Someone she cared for... Cared for very much, died on a small patch of grass by the roadside... Grass thrives on blood... That patch was always greener than the rest.

HEATHER: How sad... Have you been to your bed yet?

SAM: No. Well about ten minutes. Then the phone rang. I'll drink this tea then I'll be away to it... What are you doing with yourself today?.

HEATHER: I think I'll stay here and wait for Tony... If you need anything, bang on the bedroom wall.

A silence as they drink tea.

SAM: Tele say's its going to rain.

HEATHER: Oh, when?.

SAM: Tomorrow.

HEATHER: Oh.

SAM: Best keep out of the way tomorrow love.

HEATHER: Why?

SAM: Lad was due to be wed.... Be better if he were left alone.

HEATHER: Why?

SAM: He loves her... Despite his anger .

HEATHER: Yes.

SAM: And you'd like him to stop?

HEATHER: *(Laughs lightly)* Stop what?

SAM: Loving her...

HEATHER: Don't be silly. Why should I want that?

SAM: Drink your tea love... These things take time.

They drink as the lights slowly fade down.

End of Scene 1

ACT II Scene 2

Saturday night. Just after midnight.

Everything is as it were. Heather is asleep in the chair.

Sam enters. He nudges her awake gently.

SAM: Heather love . . . Wake up love . . . Come on sleepy head.

HEATHER: *(Awakes)* Tony?... Oh, it's you Dad... I must have nodded off.

SAM: Yes, something like that... Come on love, come home and get to your
proper bed.

HEATHER: No... I'm waiting....

SAM: Waiting for Tony! Yes I know.. But you've been sitting here all day and all of last night too...

HEATHER: He'll come back... I want... I want to be here when he does.

SAM: Why?

HEATHER: I don't know why.

SAM: Don't you love?

HEATHER: I'm worried for him. That's all.

SAM: That's all?... *(A long pause)* You're in love with him, aren't you?

HEATHER: *(Looks up then down again quickly)* No.

SAM: *(Kindly)* Funny how your "no" always sound like a "yes".

HEATHER: *(Softly)* Yes.

SAM: *(Crouches beside her, takes her hand)* I'm pleased for you... Love is the best feeling one can have in this life... The worst is hate... But hate is the child of love... Don't give birth to it... Try your damnedest not to.

HEATHER: I don't understand.

SAM: He loves her... You realise that, don't you?

HEATHER: *(Softly)* Yes, but she...

SAM: Doesn't love him?... That's not important... He can't see that at the moment... No more than he can see you... It hurts... Being invisible... It can turn love into hate... And that's bad.

HEATHER: *(Tearful)* He likes me... He said so.

SAM: Heather.

HEATHER: He called me his little soldier...

SAM: *(Smiles, stands)* You're everybody's soldier love. Fighting a war you cannot win. *(Leans over, kisses her brow)* Come on. Let's go home. You'll feel better after a good night's sleep.

HEATHER: I'm staying... I don't know why... I don't... But I have this feeling he's on his way... And I can't leave the house unlocked...

SAM: *(Moves to exit)* A little soldier guarding the fort. *(Turns back)* Have you eaten since last night?

HEATHER: Bits and pieces.

SAM: I'll bet... Look. Tell you what. I'll go and do us some egg and chips. We'll have a midnight feast. Like we did while your Mama was ill... We used to talk then love... Haven't done that for quite a time, have we? *(Exits)*

She sits quietly looking at the door. Her next speech is charged with a soft emotion as she struggles to hold back tears. It is no matter if she fails.

HEATHER: No Dad, we haven't... Not since.... Not since... Scrambled eggs on toast and a mug of cocoa... Mama... Mama... We haven't called you that... Since... Since.... *(Stands, moves around, arms wrapped around body)* So silent... Mama... Silent for days... I miss you Mama... Day after day... Silent... Looking at the stain on the ceiling above you... Remember... Memories... Running along the beach... The wind lifting your long black hair... Like the mane of a fairy tale horse... Your lovely black hair.... Cocoa and eggs... "Help me Sam"... The last sounds.... Loud.... Pleading to the one you loved most... "Help me Sam".... Cocoa and eggs... Painful screams.... "Sam. Sam".... Hands over ears Mama... On the floor, crying into eggs and cocoa... I don't want to hear Mama... I didn't... And eggs are so yellow... "Help me Sam"... Did you Dad... Did you?.... Did you help Mama?

The telephone rings. Picks up receiver.

Hello.... No Mr Banks, I'm afraid he's not. He's not been home since... Police!... *(Upset)* No... When?.... No. He's not here... Where is he Mr Banks?... But.... How bad?... I'm waiting for him. Yes... Will the police... Yes... If he arrives I'll tell him... Yes Mr Banks... Goodnight... No. I suppose it's not. *(Replaces receiver. Softly)* Tony... Tony... How could you do that if you love her? *(Sits. A noise in the hall)* Tony?...

TONY enters. He is a mess. His shirt front is blood stained and his hands are bruised and covered in dried blood. There is bruising on his face. She stands quickly and moves to him.

Tony... Tony...

TONY: What are... You....

HEATHER: I've been waiting for you. Your...

TONY: *(Sharply)* Why?

HEATHER: Everyone has been so concerned...

TONY: *(Angry)* Why?... Why?... I don't need your concern.

HEATHER: I'm sorry.

TONY: *(Softly)* Must put my hands in warm water... Hurt like hell.

HEATHER: Sit down... I'll get you a bowl. *(Moves to exit)*

TONY: *(Sits)* Aren't you going to ask me?

HEATHER: Ask what?

TONY: *(Indicating hands)* About this.

HEATHER: I know... Your father rang. *(Exits)*

TONY: *(Stands with difficulty, moves to kitchen exit)* How did he know?

HEATHER: *(Off)* The police have been to see him.

TONY: The police!

HEATHER: *(Off)* Yes... Your father wants you to ring him in the morning...
(Enters with bowl. Places it onto coffee table)

TONY: The police!... *(Sits, puts hands into water. Winces)* Oh Jesus.

HEATHER: *(Sits)* Are they sore?

TONY: What do you think... What did they say?

HEATHER: I suppose they were going to arrest you... I don't know.

TONY: Arrest me!

HEATHER: Your father said you were not to worry... Said he was able to deal
with it... Apparently, someone in the police owes him one...

TONY: Oh... God, they're sore.

HEATHER: Where have you been?

TONY: Been going crazy, that's where I've been.

HEATHER: I've been so worried... Where were you last night?

TONY: I got drunk... Stayed with a friend... Why should you be worried?...

HEATHER: *(Softly)* Soldiers do worry.

TONY: Pardon?

HEATHER: *(Stands)* That shirt ought to go into water... Or it will....

TONY: Spoil?... Everything spoils eventually... *(Takes hands out of water.
Trembles, resisting his emotions. Stands, moves away)* I should be up there.
(Looks up to the ceiling) It would have been all over by now... The loving
couple... First night... Bridal suite... Without a bed... Without a bride... Did
you know today was the big day?

HEATHER: *(Sits)* Yes.

TONY: Last night... I went to her house. Sat outside in the car... Sat there an hour. Thinking. How to do it. How to kill her... That was not the answer. It would only make things worse. I wanted her back. I had to play it right.

HEATHER: So you went to the pub?

TONY: Yes... Had a lot of thinking to do.

HEATHER: And a lot of drinking!

TONY: Drown my sorrows.

HEATHER: Did it work?

TONY: For a while, yes. I woke up this morning and said "Sod her. Sod them all. Plenty more fish in the sea". Jack, that's my mate, said "Enjoy yourself".... We went to a nightclub tonight.

HEATHER: To get drunk?

TONY: Yes. What would you have done?

HEATHER: The same, I suppose.

TONY: *(Stands. Moves around)* It didn't work... Of all the places to pick... Jack always said "Norwich is the biggest village in Norfolk". He was right... I turned around and there she was... With this bloke... Only inches from me... And he kissed her... She was mine... Mine... And he was kissing her... She saw me... She whispered to him... Laughed... Turned away... I couldn't bear her turning away... He looked... Stepped over those inches... "Sorry old man", he said... Sorry?... Sorry?... Stuck up ponce...

HEATHER: And you hit him?

TONY: *(Upset)* Yes... And her... *(Holds up his hands)* Next thing I knew it seemed as though everyone in the room was hitting me.... I ran... I just ran... Oh Jesus... What have I done... What have I done...

HEATHER: She's in hospital.

TONY: Oh God.

HEATHER: You've broken her nose, amongst other things.

TONY: *(Sits, puts head in his hands)* Oh God... I'm an animal... A bloody animal and now I've lost her.

NOTE: The following dialogue and action leads into the title of the play. It is a very tender moment and should be treated as such to achieve maximum effect. It is based on the principle of a mother's attention to a child who has fallen, her loving touch heals all pain and discomfort.

HEATHER: Perhaps... Perhaps it's for the best...

TONY: *(Loud)* The best? The best?...

HEATHER: She didn't love you, Tony.

TONY: But I love her.

HEATHER: Yes.

TONY: You have no idea how I'm feeling...

HEATHER: I might.

TONY: No. How could you... You told me... Never been hurt... Not loving anyone...

HEATHER: Aren't I?...

TONY: Not that I know of.

HEATHER: *(Stands)* No... You don't know... Do you?... *(TONY looks at her. It dawns)*

TONY: No... No... Heather... Don't. *(Holds out his hands)* Look at these... This is what I'm like... This is the kind of person I am... This is what I give to people who love me.

HEATHER: But she didn't.

TONY: But I do.

HEATHER: *(Sadly)* Yes, you do. *(Turns towards exit)*

TONY: Heather.

HEATHER: Yes Tony.

TONY: Don't go.

HEATHER: It's late... I've been here far too long... Far too long.

A silence.

You've got blood on your nose.

He wipes it away.

Is your face sore too?

TONY: Yes... Just a bit.

HEATHER: Try this.

She slowly touches the bruise with her fingers. His eyes close slowly as she moves her fingers over the bruise. She lifts her fingers away and moves sadly to the exit. He opens his eyes. Touches his face.

TONY: It's.... It's... What did you do?..

HEATHER: *(Tearfully)* Nothing. *(A sob breaks)* It was just... Just a loving touch.

A silence. He stands.

TONY: Heather.

HEATHER: *(With difficulty)* Yes.

TONY: I... I don't love you... But I so need someone to love me.

She moves slowly to him. Looks up. Smiles weakly.

HEATHER: That's good enough for me.

He takes her hands. Almost in slow motion they move closer. Her eyes close as he moves his face close to kiss her. SAM enters with two plates of egg and chips.

SAM: Service with a smile... Oh... Am I interrupting something?...

They break apart.

HEATHER: No... Yes...

SAM: Right. Well... Supper for two. *(Places plates onto coffee table. Mimics a butler)* Will you be requiring candles, sir?

TONY: *(Embarrassed)* No... Mr... Sam...

SAM: No need to explain, sir... That's what the mornings are for... I shall return to the kitchen forthwith. *(Moves to exit)*

TONY: Sam... Before you go...

SAM: Yes sir...

TONY: Would you tell me something?

SAM: I will endeavour to oblige, sir.

TONY: How do you know my Mother so well?

SAM: *(Dropping the butler voice)* Before I was a nurse, son, I was a milkman... My round took in Newmarket Road. Your mother, Milly, was not like the rest of them. Her nose stayed at the same level as mine... I'd call in for a coffee... and a chat... Mondays and Thursdays... We were good friends for a while...

TONY: Oh, I see.... And Dad didn't know?

SAM: No... Women who make friends with the milkman usually keep it to themselves... *(Pause)* I'll leave you to your supper and such.

HEATHER: *(Takes Tony's hand)* Dad, would you mind if...

SAM: No love, don't say it... Goodnight... See you in the morning. *(Exits)*

HEATHER and TONY turn to face each other, he takes her other hand.

TONY: In the morning?

HEATHER: In the morning.

She kisses him lightly on the lips.

THE END

"LOVE WITHOUT PAIN IS NOT LOVE"

THANK YOU DENNIS, THANK YOU SUSAN.

PROPERTIES LIST

ACT I Scene 1

Dust Sheets
Paste Board
Teapot
Electric Kettle
Coffee mugs
Milk Carton
Bag of sugar

Biscuits
Paste bucket
Paint brushes
Tea chest
Ply board
Step ladders
Blue wallpaper *(5 of)*
Teapot *(Sam)*
Mugs - 2 of *(Sam)*
Tin of white gloss paint
Building Society book
Handbag
Cups and saucers *(2 of)*
Cushions *(2 of)*

ACT I Scene 2

Drinking glasses *(2 of)*
Whisky bottle
Magazines
Photograph album
Loose photographs
Chinese take-away meal
Personal card *(Billy)*

ACT II Scene 1

Small carriage clock
General furniture
Various ornaments etc.
Black trousers *(Tony)*
Black shoes *(Tony)*
Ironing board
Iron
White shirt *(Tony)*
Curtain cord *(Heather)*
Mirror
Handkerchief *(Tony)*

Comb *(Tony)*
Linen basket
Unironed linen
Suitcase *(Cathy)*
Telephone
Kitchenware
Telephone Directory
Shopping bag *(Milly)*
Package *(Milly)*
Footstool
Writing paper
Pencil
Tea tray

ACT II Scene 2

Blood stained shirt *(Tony)*
Plastic bowl
Plate of egg and chips *(2 of)*

LIGHTING PLOT

ACT I Scene 1

General lighting. The impression being that there are no drapes up the window.

(Page 22) **TONY**: They'll love you, eventually... *Fade to half light.*

(Page 23) **TONY**: Put that light on will you... *Fade up to full.*

(Page 31) **TONY**: Please love me... *Fade down to two spots.*

ACT I Scene 2

(Opening of scene) Two spots. Fade up to full light on Heather's exit.

ACT II

General room lighting but as the room is now furnished it should be softer.

(Pink and orange gels)